Stephanie Snow
23 N. Park Ave
Shrewsbury, NJ 07702-4413

The Healing Journey
Volume II

HEALING and YOUR EMOTIONAL LIFE

Rev. Gerald P. Ruane, Ph.D.

Sacred Heart Press — Caldwell, New Jersey

The Scriptural quotations in this publication are from the New American Bible, 1970, used here by permission of the Confraternity of Christian Doctrine, copyright owner.

Copyright 1986
Sacred Heart Press
60 Roseland Avenue
Caldwell, New Jersey 07006
201-226-7111

DEDICATION

This volume is dedicated to Jesus Christ who is the Lord of the Sacred Heart Institute and all its ministries.

ACKNOWLEDGEMENTS

I want to acknowledge the many people who have helped me in the preparation of this volume. Especially deserving of mention are all the people of the Sacred Heart Institute and of the Association of Christian Therapists who had a share in the writing of this book.

Four people deserve special mention: Sister Ruthann Williams, O.P., who was editorial assistant, graphic designer, and typist; Sister Lois Curry, O.P., who proofread and facilitated many things; Dr. Marie Gatza who offered guidance and insight; and my own sister Mrs. Nancy Aylward for helping me at every stage of writing.

Gerald Patrick Ruane

THE HEALING JOURNEY

Volume II
Healing And Your Emotional Life

Preface i

Summary of Volume I 1

General Overview

    Chapter I
        Your Emotional Life 7

First Section

    Introduction 53

    Chapter 2
        Freedom from Fears through Faith
        Which Focuses on Jesus 55

    Chapter 3
        Anger as Power for the Kingdom . 83

    Recapitulation 106

Second Section

    Introduction 107

    Chapter 4
        Grief: A Timely Grace 109

    Recapitulation 139

Concluding Remarks 141

Appendices

   A. Sacred Heart Institute
      Audio Cassettes 142

   B. Professional Healing
      Organizations 145

   C. Further Reading 146

PREFACE

The main job of the author is to be like a person who runs a fruit stand. He sells you the fruit; he doesn't chew it for you. This book seeks to present the material to you, but not to chew or digest it for you. That pleasure is yours.

Like Volume I (and volumes still to come), this book attempts to be pastoral, not pedantic; concrete rather than abstract; focused on particular aspects of the healing journey; and positive in its outlook.

In this volume I will be sharing with you the experiences and battles I have undergone in my attempt to live free of some of the negative emotions in my life. People have urged me not to make this just another book of theory, but one with plenty of practical experiences. So writing this book was hard work because I am still personally working on lots of these areas in my own life. I have tried to share the struggles and not just the victories. And, above all, I have tried to share with the reader the perspective that these struggles are not ones we carry on alone, but rather in and with the Lord Jesus. It is to him that any credit for battles won is due.

If some of the autobiographical details are not terribly meaningful to you, skip over them and move on. Many people have mentioned that personal sharings have been helpful to them, and so I decided to continue that approach.

Return to the first image on this page and consider this book a fruit stand. Take what appeals to you and leave the rest for another time when it may have more meaning for you. Take in what you can easily digest. Leave the rest for later. Come back for more when you feel the need.

As I have said in Volume I, our healing journey is an exciting adventure and worth whatever commitment is necessary in time and resources. It is a very serious undertaking, but one which need not be a crushing burden. Why not go to your favorite place: the beach, a lake, the woods or mountains (either literally or figuratively) and relax. Read a few pages; and then let God direct your mind and heart.

This book should not be read at one sitting. It has to be ingested and digested at one's own pace and preference. "One day at a time" is a good way to live our lives. As we take each day as it comes, we need to maintain a healthy balance and make certain that there's plenty of time for play, prayer, work and rest. The last two usually get sufficient attention; but some improvement is generally called for in the play and/or prayer areas.

May your reading of this book help to improve the quality of your prayer time and give greater meaning and zest to your play. May the work and rest parts of your day be enhanced by the healing of your emotional life.

SUMMARY OF VOLUME I

Volume I of the series <u>The Healing Journey</u> is titled "Overcoming Obstacles to Healing." While familiarity with this first volume is not absolutely necessary for the reading of this book, a brief outline may help to orient the reader to some basic concepts and suppositions.

<u>A Brief Outline</u>

The first section of Volume I centered on Jesus and how we understand and relate to him.

Jesus is the Healer and we are his helpers. He is the Messiah and he does the saving and healing. He can and will use us on his healing team if we understand and keep the order straight in our minds and hearts.

Tensions can be an obstacle to Jesus' healing love and so we must release them to Jesus.

We must change our way of thinking and accept that healing is an on-going evolutionary process, a life-long journey with many healings of various kinds all along the way.

We also need to see more clearly how Jesus is healing right now and not spend our time waiting for some magic moment, minister, or instrument to arrive upon the scene.

The second section introduced the idea of the Orphan Complex and the Lord's remedy

for it which is to invite us to share his Father's love. (Chapters five and six)
    The remaining two chapters considered the topic of forgiveness; our need to receive it on the one hand (Chapter seven) and to give it freely with the other hand (Chapter eight). A priest friend delights in saying that "God gives us forgiveness <u>for giving</u>" that same forgiveness to those who have hurt us.

<u>A</u> <u>More</u> <u>Detailed</u> <u>Summary</u>

    A longer and more detailed chapter by chapter summary is presented now with the hope that it will deepen the reader's appreciation of the material already covered.

First Section

    Chapter One stressed that Jesus is the Healer, but that all baptized Christians are called to be his helpers, a part of his team no matter how unworthy we seem or feel. As we focus on him, our Healer and our Hope, we will learn how to fulfill our role in this ministry.
    In Chapter Two we considered the need to give all our tensions to Jesus, to relax in his love, and to let him do what he wants in us and in others at his own pace and timing. We live under such tension that we need to learn ways to relax with the Lord and let him love us to new and deeper life.
    Chapter Three cautioned that "once may

not be enough." We are called to be patient as Jesus leads us to full life - a life of healing and wholeness. Healing is a <u>process</u> which covers every part and stage of our growth and development as human beings, touched by God's power and love.

In our human folly we often want the Lord to heal according to our specifications and timetable. He, in his perfect love, does not commit such a blunder. He, the only Healer, heals when he knows it is proper and in the best possible way so that the healing will last. The Lord is interested in our being whole, but he is interested primarily in our coming to live with him one day forever.

A cancer specialist recently mentioned that there are two cases in which he could say that God had performed a miracle of complete healing. In both cases those who had been healed have strayed away from God despite all that he has done for them. They missed the greater healings. The Lord wants us to keep our eyes on him. He does want to make us whole, but his idea of wholeness and ours are often two different things.

His is the long-range view, the view from eternity, so often we are called upon to wait patiently to see what his love "hath wrought" in our lives. A true story may help. A priest had such a severe case of shingles that he was almost blinded in one eye. God's love came to him through the doctors and nurses and their medication, and also through his friends and relatives. Because those people were willing to let

God use them, the priest experienced a deep inner healing which also speeded his physical recovery. In God's loving plan the healing that was going on within him emotionally was much more important than the physical healing. If he had been centered so much on Jesus' healing him instantaneously of the shingles, he might not have been open to the deeper, more important healing which the Lord wanted to accomplish in his life.

The final chapter of this section highlighted the fact that Jesus is healing his people right <u>now</u>. The Lord is working in our lives at every moment and we have to be alert to his presence so as not to miss what he is doing.

Second Section

The second section came to grips with the nitty-gritty of overcoming obstacles and eliminating some negatives from our lives.

The Orphan Complex is a common phenomenon in which people walk around looking, speaking, and acting like orphans, no matter what they might say or seem. (Chapter five)

Jesus delights in sharing his Father with us and that's the only way the Orphan Within comes to an evolutionary certitude about <u>who</u> he/she is because of <u>whose</u> he/she is. With that knowledge comes maturity.

Jesus comes to us and says, "I love you and I want to heal you of that deep,

deep complex which says you do not belong, that you do not have a father. I want to show you my Father and your Father, my God and your God." The Lord has revealed the Father to us in many ways. In the scriptures he talks about his Father and our Father (Jn 20:17). He gives us parables, such as the prodigal son (Lk 15:11-32) which is really a story of a father so prodigal that he just keeps pouring out his love and his forgiveness in a limitless way. God is also described as that conscientious shepherd (Mt 18:10-14) who lets none of us stray away without seeking us out and bringing us back into the safety of his love. (Chapter six)

Forgiveness is vital. We have Jesus' word for it. We need to receive forgiveness from God, from others, and from ourselves to have a good life. (Chapter seven)

And we need to give forgiveness to God, others, and yes, even to ourselves, if we are to have a full life. (Chapter eight)

The first volume concludes with three appendices:

A. What is a Healing Mass?

B. Twelve Spiritual Push-Ups

C. Further Reading on Healing

CHAPTER I

YOUR EMOTIONAL LIFE

"There is an appointed time for everything; and a time for every affair under the heavens . . . a time to weep and a time to laugh; a time to mourn, and a time to dance."
(Ecc 3:1,4)

"God, grant me the serenity to accept the things I cannot change, courage to change the things I can, and wisdom to know the difference."

There are almost as many definitions of emotional health as there are emotions. Whatever definition fits your idea of emotional health might form your working definition. A working definition is one that doesn't have to be infallible or set in cement. It just seems right for you, which is not to insinuate in any way that it is all relative. But I am suggesting that emotional health will have variations of meaning and application, and any of the definitions given are workable ones. Why not choose one, or combine two or more into your own working definition?

Thinking About It

Emotional health is the ability to love and be loved. Actually, we should reverse the order because we need to feel and accept love before giving it. If we have been loved, cherished, and desired from the very moment of our existence, then we are often exceptionally healthy emotionally and otherwise.

Another definition holds that emotional health is making the appropriate response to circumstances and the stages of one's life: the people, places, structures, institutions, etc.

A third attempt sees it as the state in which a person is functioning in proper order and alignment of body, mind, and spirit. Emotions are given as much importance as the intellectual, physical, spiritual, and social components of the human being.

Another definition says that emotional health is peace and balance, that state of being in which we are not only aware of possessing emotions, but have integrated them into our total lives. We have invited emotional feelings to the banquet of our lives, seated them in a place of honor, and made them part of the total picture.

Other people see emotional health as the state in which we are attempting to know and love ourselves and to move on to deeper stages of growth. In this definition emotions are seen to be as important as the other parts of our beings. Not more important nor less important, but as important.

Someone may object that emotions don't really need to be recognized, that they will make themselves known and demand our attention. Why wait until the crisis arrives? Recognition and acceptance are tremendously vital elements in emotional health.

Go For The Connection

My favorite definition explains emotional health as making and keeping a <u>clear connection</u>. With whom? With God, myself, and others. In many of the twelve-step programs, the literature speaks about the addict using the substance or person to whom he is addicted and saying: "Please, connect with me and make me whole." (We will discuss more about these twelve-step programs later.) It never happens except for the briefest interval and then comes the fall back into the pit of despair.

Each of us is a unity of body, mind, and spirit. We are whole, not in any absolute or completely realized sense, but in a relative but nonetheless true sense. Some people talk or act as if they were only half a person, looking for another to make them whole and complete. That's a very serious misconception and leads to enormous harm.

Wholeness and holiness, health and healing are the result of making and keeping the proper connections with ourselves and every part of ourselves. In the process we are also connecting with our neighbors.

As children we learn about and catch emotional health from others. We find a sense of security and self-esteem; and also gain the ability to deal with complex inner problems if we are treated with respect. When we are given well-defined standards of values plus guidance in how to achieve them, we develop high self-esteem. This is based on the quantity and quality of respectful, accepting and concerned treatment we have received from significant people in our lives: parents, teachers, and others.

People with high self-esteem expect to succeed and to be liked by others and both usually happen. People with low self-esteem are easily discouraged, feel isolated, unloved and unlovable. They often do not succeed and are frequently not liked by others since they do not like themselves.

Many individuals with low self-esteem have experienced rejection from significant people in their lives and that has opened them to feelings of self-rejection. The struggle with self-rejection is a serious one. Consider the following story.

"A man was describing a sense of futility he felt when reaching out to others for intimacy. At one point, he related an event from his boyhood. He had grown up in a small mid-western town. On the day of his birth, one other boy was delivered in the little hospital located there. He explained how, throughout his boyhood, whenever he performed disappointingly, his father remarked: 'I must have brought the wrong boy home from the hospital.' When things got really tough for him, he would dream of what his 'real' parents were like, and how loving they probably were.

"Many of us could tell similar stories. At work here is the familiar mechanism of conditional love; i.e., people love me only when I do well. Conditional love is a time-bomb ready to go off at the slightest touch. While desperately reaching out to others, such a person easily can have a deep conviction that it is a useless effort. Who wants to spend a lifetime earning love?

"And very subtly, he can communicate to others that he expects to be rejected. He will even manipulate others to reject him. Like a grim scorekeeper, such a person will add name after name to the list of those who have backed away. 'You see, people don't want me!' A kind of emotional numbness sets in and, to ease the pain, work becomes an all-consuming antidote, until one day the person breaks down physically or sinks into depression.

"The feeling of self-rejection is awakened by demands and pressures which society puts on the individual and to which the individual is unknowingly conditioned to respond. . . . The responses are based on childhood decisions made when we were terribly young, fearful, and lacking the context necessary to evaluate our difficult experiences. As adults we have the freedom to change our decisions, and the experience to make better ones. Unfortunately, many people are unaware that they now have the choice or are too overwhelmed to use it."[1]

But there is always hope for improvement and healing because time, insight and prayer can help the situation. Prayer for inner healing is a vital tool in healing the wounds of self-rejection because such prayer takes the individual to the heart and person of Jesus. In company with the Lord, the person goes back to the events which precipitated the wound. The presence of Jesus, our living Lord and present Friend, changes the emotional context of that incident. The individual then sees and feels it in a new light and is able to face the various emotional responses he felt at the time of the original incident.

In Seasons And Stages

Greater growth usually takes place after a crisis such as the ones we have just mentioned. Humans reach the final stages of "integration" somewhere in their 50's or later. As one ages, life may get more difficult, but also it gets better. Life is not like an arch, inevitably going down after the mid-thirties or forties.

"Life is a journey of growth and development. At each stage God is with us, loving us 100%, even as he loved his Son, Jesus. On this journey, we experience many emotions, all of which can help us grow. We experience aloneness as Jesus did when he cried, 'My God, why have you forsaken me?' but this aloneness too passes into greater maturity, understanding and new life. So too with our sinfulness, our brokenness, our depression, our self-willed projects that were improperly rooted. All are part of the life-expression of growth."2

All these can and will be healed and redeemed if and as we say "yes" to the journey of growth and development (our healing journey). The next section may clarify some areas of confusion.

A Healthy Emotional Life

A healthy emotional life may be seen as resting on two foundations: <u>prayer</u> and <u>relationship</u>.
<u>Prayer</u> means <u>connecting with God</u> through meditation, reflection, contemplation, quiet time, or whatever you want to call it. It is the real me meeting the real God.
<u>Relationship</u> means <u>connecting with other human beings</u> as well as myself. It signifies striving for community, reaching out to help and touch, asking for and giving intimacy. It means feeling comfortable with myself and my sisters and brothers in God's family. It also means helping them to feel comfortable with me.

Prayer

Prayer takes time and effort, but both are worth it. Prayer doesn't happen overnight, but it begins to improve as the person perseveres and is as open as possible with God. The "real me" takes a lot of coaxing to reveal, and the "real God" wants to reveal himself; but one has to stop, look, and listen reverently and repeatedly. All of that means a substantial commitment and effort.

How can we pray? Pray freely and lovingly in words, psalms, snatches of favorite hymns or meaningful silences. Pray with your body - in any position you find helpful. Pray with your heart and soul, and pray in the Spirit always. Pray for all that God our Father wants to give to you at this special moment. Pray prudently, attentive to what you are feeling. Your silence may say more than the most eloquently spoken prayer.

Prayer is not a plunge into a morass of self-pity. It is not the recitation of words well-said but little-meant, like children in a play mouthing lines with little sense of their meaning.

Prayer is turning from self to God and entering into communion with him in every way we can. Prayer is recognizing how much we need God and responding to the fact that he is present to us at all times.3

If you seek a satisfying and even exciting life of prayer, you need the following ingredients:

1. a Hunger deep within for the things of God and of the Spirit;
2. a Determination to find the Spirit and to follow his leadings;
3. Perseverance in the effort; and

4. a Commitment to love.

A Love That Endured

Blessed Edith Stein had all four ingredients. A German Jew, she was a famous philosopher, a convert to Catholicism, and finally a Carmelite nun. She was killed at Auschwitz in 1942. Before she was so brutally exterminated by the Nazis she shared her feelings with a Jesuit friend, Father Herschmann. Over thirty-five years later he spoke about her.

"But Edith Stein was not only a Jew lovingly united to the Jewish people; she was also a German united to the German people. And, as such, she was constantly faced with the question: 'Who will atone for what is happening to the Jewish people in the name of the German people?' It caused her intense suffering that baptized Christians like Hitler and Himmler were taking the guilt of such awful crimes upon themselves. 'Who will turn this enormous guilt into a blessing for both peoples?' Ultimately the answer she came to was that only the victims of hatred could do it, if instead of letting their wounds produce new hatred, they would be willing to carry the suffering of their fellow victims and tormentors.

"I will never forget the conversations I had with this genuinely Christian philosopher when time and again she would insist that hatred must never be given the last word. Somehow it had to be possible - through prayer and atonement - to obtain the grace of conversion for those who hated. Hadn't Jesus, when he prayed for those who hated him, those who crucified and pierced him, turned his wounds into the symbol of love that proved to be stronger in the end?

There is no question that Auschwitz will always remain for us as a terrifying revelation of the destructive potential of human lovelessness. But there is another revelation at Auschwitz, infinitely transcending the first: that the love which endures the Cross and wounds ultimately overcomes all lovelessness. This is the love that says to the Cross: For the sake of the love which has come to us through Jesus' Cross and wounds, I love you and I testify - hate is not stronger than love."[4]

Few of us will face the extreme test that Blessed Edith Stein met and overcame. Nonetheless, there will be tests for each of us and we need to prepare for them as she did by a strong and active prayer life. In seeking a stronger and more balanced prayer life, a Spiritual Director is an invaluable if not indispensable asset. The director listens to your words and to the movements of the heart and shares what the Lord is revealing to him or her.

Relationship

We defined relationship as being connected with others as well as ourselves and mentioned striving for community, reaching out to help and touch, asking for and giving intimacy. That's a healthy relationship and building it is not an easy process. It is very hard work and takes time and practice. In the beginning our efforts at making the connection with others are usually awkward. As we keep trying, they become less so. After a while we find them very easy and natural. Truly at that stage they have become a part of us and a very healthy part, I might add.

But Not Without Pain

That phrase will be one of the constants in this book. Whatever definition of emotional health you choose, its application to your life will not be without pain. Peace, harmony and balance are achieved at considerable cost. It is good to be aware of the cost as well as the benefits of emotional health. If we are not aware of the cost involved, then the cost will be paid by others as well as ourselves.

Just remember that your goal in life is not to be angelic, but truly human and Christian. Many people have spent their lives pursuing the angelic virtues. Such efforts are doomed to fail. What is worse, such efforts detract from what should be our all-consuming task: developing and Christianizing our human lives to the fullest. Ask God to teach you the difference and help you to fulfill your destiny as a Christian man or woman. Why not stop here for just a moment and join me in this prayer?

"Thanks, God, for another day to live and move in your love and light. Grant me for this healing journey your light and your grace to follow the way to health and wholeness. Thank you for giving me the security of your love to face myself and enjoy who I am: a full human being, your beloved child."

Ecstacy

When two people build a relationship of love and friendship and share their wholeness to enrich each other and their neighbors, they know much joy and, at times, even ecstacy.

But let's talk a little more about the agony of the process before we get too taken up with the ecstacy of it.

Agony

In a relationship each individual comes with his or her own set of dreams, needs, expectations. So often these are not even understood by the person involved, and consequently they are unknown or barely perceived by the other person.

One woman married with the belief that her husband would make her happy. In the depth of her unconscious she felt that if anything made her unhappy, her husband was to blame. It was a terribly difficult situation for the man and also for the woman because of her unrealistic expectations. Luckily there was a great love there which was able to survive the hard times which resulted. That love survived and even thrived during times of therapy and counseling and prayer which were needed to heal the hurt caused by that one erroneous idea. After that they began to face, accept and surrender to the Lord the other ideas and attitudes which were hurting their relationship. All of these could be and were healed as the woman learned to surrender her mistaken idea to the healing power of the Lord's love.

In all relationships with others, balance and maturity are such vital elements. Remember that we come as whole, if wounded, persons seeking to share our wholeness with another and to accept the gifts the other offers us.

Be Aware

There are several things it will be helpful for you to be aware of.

<u>Be</u> <u>aware</u> <u>of</u> <u>infatuation</u>. There is usually some of it involved in every relationship. Enjoy it, but know it doesn't last. Moderate it, and don't let it get out of bounds.

<u>Be</u> <u>aware</u> <u>of</u> <u>neurotic</u> <u>dependency</u> whereby you make the other person an idol, the source and fountain of all good things. Neurotic dependency occurs when the person

enters into a relationship and sees the other person as the beginning and end of all happiness.

<u>Be</u> <u>aware</u> <u>of</u> <u>projection</u>. We project onto another person what we cannot accept in ourselves, those feelings, those qualities which don't fit in with our understanding of who we are. Oftentimes a man will deny his feminine qualities of tenderness, warmth, nurturing, and project them onto a woman. He will even marry her because of these qualities. Then he expects her to be the complete embodiment of all these attributes, which of course she cannot be. When he discovers this he feels betrayed because the woman is "less" than he imagined and does not live up to that perfection he once "saw" in her. To be healed the man will need to identify the projection, face it, and ask the Lord to help him so that he may see in himself those very beautiful qualities he has been projecting onto his wife. In the process he will come to see her with her own special gifts and qualities and will begin to appreciate her for who she really is.

<u>Be</u> <u>aware</u> <u>of</u> <u>excessive</u> <u>gift</u> <u>giving</u>. Are you feeling uneasy about the gifts the other is giving you? Or are you uneasy about the gifts you are giving? Check up on what is going on. Is this a subtle or not so subtle form of competition between the two of you? Is there a desire to dominate or control? Are you afraid of not being "loved" unless you shower the other with presents? In any case, why not begin to

talk to the other about this situation? Don't accuse or judge. Share your feelings of discomfort. Clarify and verify and try to do both in a conducive atmosphere and at a propitious time.

    <u>Be</u> <u>aware</u> <u>of</u> <u>the</u> <u>need</u> <u>for</u> <u>tough</u> <u>love</u>. At times in a relationship, one party may accuse the other of some offense without any effort at verification. "Do this or else" is the ultimatum. The reaction to that is often, "Goodbye and good riddance." That, however, doesn't save the relationship. The person may be a fine human being but with a great need to be in control always or to be perfectly right all the time.

    In this, as in every other case, love has to be the context in which we act; but it doesn't have to be a saccharin, sentimental, marshmallow type love. It has to be tough love. It's the same type of tough love that parents learn to use with their children who are experiencing various addictions or negative behavior patterns. Tough love is gutsy love, the type that lays down its life for a beloved.

    In this case tough love means seeking to share the truth of one's perceptions and persevering with the other person until he can hear and accept another side of the story.

    <u>Be</u> <u>aware</u> <u>that</u> <u>you</u> <u>can</u> <u>choose</u> <u>to</u> <u>hang</u> <u>in</u>. Take the case of a man in his late 40's who always wanted a son but never had one. Then one day a young man appeared who just lost his father and was yearning to have

someone to take his place. A beautiful relationship developed. They enjoyed each other's company and their interests and families matched very well. As their relationship deepened expectations and demands were made. A serious rift occurred. They decided to take a vacation from each other to let the dust settle. Each person agreed to revive the network of friends and relatives which they had begun to neglect.

It wasn't easy, but it was good because when they returned each was able to see his responsibility in the misunderstanding and also his potential for making a contribution to what promised to be a much healthier friendship. They began the reconciliation with the help of a counselor. They needed time to express their hurts, to explain their reasons for having acted as they had, and to gain insights into their own behavior and that of the other party. With prayer, good sense, and a little humor, they were able to move to the next step which was to begin meeting socially. Later on they began doing more things together and resumed their sharing and caring. It was not so intense nor so demanding; but it became a very solid and rewarding friendship.

Thank God they were willing to take the chance of relating and growing and that they were mature enough to realize that they had to do something to save the relationship. Thank God they endured the separation (vacation) and then came back to begin to build a better relationship brick by brick.

A Mistaken Notion

Many Christians have the idea that they have to be perfect. For some reason - whether it be training, heredity or environment - they bought the notion that they had to be perfect human beings, perfect followers of Christ.

Where to place the blame for that mistaken notion isn't clear. Some of it is the responsibility of those who trained us and some is undoubtedly our own fault. It really doesn't matter who's to blame because we have to face that belief here and now and see it for what it is: an impossible burden. When all is said and done (and there is usually much more said than done), we know that we can never be perfect. In fact, being perfect would, I am sure, be a great surprise and an equally great trial to all our friends and relatives. Furthermore, if we were perfect, we wouldn't need Jesus as Lord anymore. We could and would do it on our own.

When the Lord judges us, it will not be on how perfect we appeared, but on how we have tried to love him, ourselves, and our neighbor. The standard of judgment will not be our perfection, thank God; but our perseverance with his grace despite failures and sins.

Judged On Love

We will be judged by Love itself, and we will be judged on how we tried to love.

So what do we do when we face our failures? For face them, we must. Personally I know that I have not been able to help all those who came to me. In some cases I have actually damaged people, not deliberately, but because I tried to do it on my own or almost on my own, giving Jesus only an occasional nod or two.

Jesus points out in his parable how the Good Samaritan (Lk 10:33) was <u>moved with compassion</u> when he helped the wounded and beaten Jew. How often we Christians can be moved by <u>compassion</u> to help someone who is wounded and beaten, but at times our <u>own passion</u> may get in the way. It may be our passion for perfection or fame, security or love, intimacy or whatever. The result can often be harmful to the person we are seeking to help.

As a spiritual director and one who prays for healing, I need to monitor myself and my feelings as I reach out to help another. It's only with God's help and that of a competent advisor that I can stay clear of some of the booby traps involved in this ministry. And even then I do not always succeed.

So what am I to do? The same thing I do with any sin or failure. Get rid of it. Not in a facile, "Oh, it's nothing really," approach, but in a serious acceptance of my failure, and a sincere act of contrition and an equally sincere act of faith in Jesus' love for me and my neighbor. "Lord, I have sinned against you. Lord, have mercy. Lord, I have sinned against my neighbor. Lord, have mercy. Lord, I have sinned against myself. Lord, have mercy."

I lay my failures at the feet of Jesus and let him take them to his cross where he will redeem them. He will write straight with crooked lines. He will make all things work out for the good. Another thing which has helped me is the realization that this is not the Last Chance Corral. My words or actions which have hurt my brother or sister are not the last words or actions which they will hear or receive. It is the Lord's work and he is not going to let his sheep be dispersed or harmed beyond repair. It's his ministry which he has shared with many of us and he will bring it to a happy end.

Perfection? No, Just Progress

God doesn't seek perfection, just progress.

"It was pointed out to me the other day that the greatest baseball player in history batted .400 which means he failed six out of ten times. Somehow that made me feel a little better about myself.

"I think we tend to focus too much on success stories - how Christians, like Homeric gods, always make it big. I confess I get tired of hearing such heroics. Emerson was right: 'Every hero gets to be a bore at last.'

"Personally, I'd like to hear a few more stories about failures like me.

"Fortunately, the Bible is full of them: Abraham lied, Moses lost his temper, Gideon lost his nerve. Peter kept putting both feet in his mouth, Paul was sometimes curt and inconsiderate, Mark went home to mother, Thomas doubted, Martha pouted. Most biblical men and women cut unheroic figures, but they're still my heroes; I need some failures to look up to now and then.

"But David is my favorite; he muffed it so many times. And yet I read that it's said of him that he was a 'godly' man. How can it be? Is there hope for a failure like me? It seems there is. It all depends on the state of the heart.

"'Godly' may put us off since the word connotes so much more than it denotes. We're inclined to think of someone sinless but the original word had nothing to do with sin. It signified one who loved the Lord and longed to be like him. The corresponding word in the New Testament is translated 'saint.'

"It seems, then, that anyone can be 'godly' - in fact, can be a 'saint' - because what matters most is not performance but the inclination of the heart. As Jesus said, 'Blessed are those who hunger and thirst after righteousness for they will be filled.' (Mt 5:6)

"God doesn't look for perfection; he knows the miserable stuff of which we're made. We 'godly' people will surely sin and just as certainly our sins will be found out. We will notice the defilement because God will show it to us. It is the sign of his presence.

"And when that sin is faced and forgiven, we, too, can go on. And going on, after all, is all that matters. God doesn't look for perfection, you see, only progress.

"C.S. Lewis wrote, 'No amount of falls will really undo us if we keep picking ourselves up each time. We shall, of course, be very muddy and tattered children by the time we reach home . . . The only fatal thing is to lose one's temper and give up.'" (Letters to Malcolm)5

One of my favorite stories concerns an ice skater who fell during an important competition. Up until the fall she had the highest score and was obviously going to win the gold medal. Her fall destroyed all that. A TV commentator with no obvious compassion grilled her on what she was thinking about while she was lying on the ice. Her reply was simple and to the point and worthy of a gold medalist in life. She said, "Getting up and finishing my routine."

A Crossroads Ministry

As we make progress on our healing journey, we often meet people and enjoy their company and friendship. The Lord frequently has brought us together to do some specific work for him. It's wonderful to experience his love and blessings on our little group or team. We would be happy to stay on our own personal Tabor with the Lord and these servants/friends of his. Then time and circumstances point toward a change. We are called to separate and go to labor in another part of the Lord's vineyard. The separation hurts and that's natural, but we must move on. Perhaps what follows will help you. It has been a gift to me.

Think about your life as a journey and see that you and your friends (on their own journey) have met at the crossroads. Rejoice in the joy of the meeting and the good that resulted. But even as you do, know that it is right and good to let them resume their journey even as you do the same. You may very well meet again down the road, and it will be very good. It will not be the same for all of you will have grown. Be sad for a time about the parting. Rejoice in the call to continue your journey with the Lord. Verily you will meet all your crossroad friends one day in heaven. The journeying will be over and the celebrating will never end.

PIES Or SPIES

Many self-help programs suggest paying attention to one's PIES; the P, physical; I, intellectual; E, emotional; and S, spiritual sides of one's life. I often shared that word with its special meanings with people who came to me. One of them remarked at a subsequent session that PIES should be changed to SPIES. He explained that he wanted to keep PIE in the middle with the same meaning, but bracket it with S's for the Spiritual and Social dimensions of life.

SPIES is not just playing around with words and letters. This is serious business because human beings are a unity of all five dimensions. Why not make a personal growth contract with yourself? It is quite a simple form to fill out. The area which may cause some difficulty is taking yourself seriously enough to want to do something to improve your life. If you can't muster the effort to do that, then are you really that serious about yourself? Somehow it seems likely that you are very interested in your emotional life if you have taken the time to read this book.

Your Own Growth Contract

A personal growth contract is made with yourself and must be taken seriously. Don't cheat yourself by undervaluing the effort you make. <u>You are worth it</u>.

Under each of the five categories - spiritual, physical, intellectual, emotional, and social - fill in a goal you want to attain. List one or two means that you are going to use to achieve your goal. Finally, give the date you'll begin and another date when you'll end. The latter is the deadline or cut off point at which you will evaluate how well you are doing, and will see if you want to continue.

The contract is not iron-clad or written in blood, but it is a very serious, sacred, and solemn agreement you make with and for yourself.

Please, plan a time for discussing the contract with your spiritual director or a mature Christian friend. In fact, I urge you to do this and give it the time it deserves. Such attention will show how important the contract is and how determined you are to be healthy in all the dimensions of your being. How faithfully you fulfill this contract will give you and your spiritual director or guide a clear indication of how serious you are about achieving healing and wholeness.

In some personal growth contracts I have seen there is a page for each dimension and a final page for any comments you might want to make. There is room for your signature and that of your advisor and a line for the date when you agreed to this contract. Sound formal and serious? It is, and I hope you treat it that way.

Homework, You Say?

Make your own SPIES chart, similar to the one shown opposite, or make up your own form. For each of the five areas - spiritual, physical, intellectual, emotional, and social - be as specific and concrete as possible. Why so much fuss about the other dimensions of our lives in a book on emotional health? Because we are so interconnected and such a unity that we need to

SPIES CHART

Goals	Means/Resources	Begin By	Completed By

have a wholistic approach to our lives. Whatever we do in one area influences for good or bad the other areas. Just think about the last time you had a serious case of the flu. You were probably physically very ill and uncomfortable. What did it do to the social, intellectual, emotional, and spiritual areas of your life?

Remember, however, as you work at your chart that Rome wasn't built in a day. Don't turn SPIES into a burden, nor create an impossible dream. Be gentle with yourself. Take it one step at a time. Rolling hills can be climbed. A mountain can defeat us before we even start by the sheer awesomeness of its height. Progress, not perfection. And certainly not overnight.

Danger Points

Beware! There are the times in all of our lives when we know we are in danger. When certain weaknesses or sensitivities are touched, when our buttons are pressed, we react. H.A.L.T. is a catchword for many. When Hungry, Angry, Lonely, or Tired, put the brakes on and come to a halt. Then take control of your life once again. Or better yet, decide to surrender that control and your life to the Lord.

Some of us have addictive or compulsive personalities with regard to food, drink, drugs, gambling, lust, and/or other things or people. Only recently have we become aware of how some persons have multiple addictions. I have known people who were addicted to alcohol, food, gambling, and lust, and were overcoming their addictions by using one of the twelve-step programs of spiritual recovery. Interestingly, success in such a program for one addiction does not automatically flow over to other addictions. The same steps or principles may be adapted, but each addiction must be faced itself.

The cost of sobriety in these areas is constant vigilance and daily contact with God and others who are fighting the same fight. The great success of AA and other such groups is the result of forming into a community people with similar problems. The group members provide support and encouragement and proclaim humbly and yet firmly: "We've been there and it has worked for us. It will work for you. Victory is possible if you give yourself to this program of spiritual recovery."

Some Practical Suggestions

In everyone's life there are situations and circumstances which are danger points. Personally, when I'm tired or rushing, I can easily snap at people. Consequently, I try to be very aware of that particular pressure. I'll never be able to avoid all of these pressures, so I have to learn to live with them. Sometimes I do express my anger inappropriately, and I normally apologize for what I have done. That's good for my humility. I'm learning how to live with, accept, and honor my emotions. I also am learning to live with my successes and failures. I'm getting better at it and feeling more comfortable about it. Believe me, it's better this way.

One thing which helps me is to slow down and connect with the Lord. Even a short prayer is enough.

Another help is to share what I am experiencing with a friend either by phone or in person.

Take An Instant Vacation

Taking an instant vacation is very good. I can't always get away from a situation physically, so I try to do so emotionally and mentally. I just sit back and realize that it will all be the same in a hundred years. If I die today things will carry on. That's not being morbid, it's just putting things in perspective. I do some breathing exercises, perhaps take a short walk around the office or my room, but preferably outside. I wash my face and hands, comb my hair and take time to smile.

Occasionally I use the following prescription to get me back into balance and out of the danger zone.

1. Write a love letter to Jesus, thanking him for all the good people and things in your life, and for all his help in your trials.

2. Reach out to the poor and less fortunate than you. No matter how poor and bad your life seems, there's usually someone worse off than you . . . and usually not

too far from you.

3. Rejoice in the Lord and let his joy and peace flow into you starting with the top of your head and enveloping every part of you. Laugh at yourself, and laugh with someone else.

Try some of these things. Write your own prescription and then follow it and adapt as you develop your own specifically tailored plan of attack. Or better yet, a plan of <u>retreat</u> to a more peaceful you.

Why not use one of the affirmations at the end of the book? Especially good is this one: I'm a child of God, therefore I love myself unconditionally. I accept God's love and know that he's taking care of me.

One Special Danger

The phrase "extreme self - reference" means that no matter what happens or what might be said, I refer it to myself regardless of what it is and/or how far removed from me it is. A person who is balding may be so sensitive that he gets angry and depressed when anyone even mentions a bald eagle. No matter what the context or how ridiculous it is, he knows "they" are making fun of him. He takes it personally and is deeply hurt.

Actually <u>extreme</u> <u>self-reference</u> is a way of saying: "I'm the center of the world and nothing happens that doesn't have a reference to me. People are always thinking and speaking about me. They can't get enough of me."

A little bit of common sense might be the best antidote for that particular type of approach to life. Just read out loud the last paragraph and see if it matches your thought patterns. Then consider what the ramifications of such patterns are. You might ask yourself the following questions:

Does the sun revolve around the moon or vice-versa? Am I trying to be the sun, or am I willing to bathe in its light? Who is on the throne in the center of my heart? Me? . . . or God? My will or his?

Falling into the trap of extreme self-reference sets you up for an abundance of hurts, and not a few fights. There will be enough of them anyway, so why go looking for more?

Dealing With Tension In A Relationship

Every dynamic organic process produces waste. This is true of every productive system, including the marvelous organism of our human body. It is also true of any relationship which is even half alive. There is waste which must be disposed of and a good discussion and confrontation can clear a lot of things away.

These are a necessary by-product of any intense, dynamic, interpersonal relationship in which two or more independent but interrelated persons attempt to negotiate their needs and expectations. There are an interesting variety of conscious and unconscious negative responses to another (as well, of course, as positive ones): disappointment, annoyance, frustration, and rage among others. These erupt at times and need to be discharged.

This flushing of the interpersonal systems enables the life-channels to continue their creative interchanges. Otherwise waste develops in the relationship, and the creative channels become polluted. Then the poison of unresolved anger will suffuse the entire human exchange. An honest, moderate, and controlled expression of anger is far better than endless emotional constipation.6

All of our feelings are our friends. Anger is our friend. If it signals that we are unhappy, why not pay attention to it, just as we pay attention to the little red light on the dashboard of our car that lets us know something is wrong? Ignoring one's anger can be as foolish as ignoring the presence of the flu or a fever. Recognizing the anger and discussing it with someone - the other person, a friend, a counselor, a clergyperson - are the first steps in resolving the problem and will help rebuild the relationship.

If the event which has created the tensions is not fatal for the relationship, a resolution will most likely come. Out of the discussion and confrontation may emerge a new understanding, a new forgiveness, and a promise and contract to guard against that sort of thing's happening again. Hopefully, it will follow that pattern. If you need help in this area or any other one, why not consider the following two sections very carefully?

Is Therapy For You?

Going into or resuming therapy can be a little frightening and humbling. It will not, however, be fatal and often can be quite helpful. I encourage you to seek therapy from a competent professional if any of the following have happened or are happening.
1. You have thought about therapy several times but never have gotten around to it.
2. Some of your recent behavior points in that direction.
3. Your life is out of control in one area and you are not coping in other areas as well as you might want to.
4. You are experiencing low levels of fear, anger, grief, or guilt, but almost constantly; and you don't seem to have a clue about how to handle it alone. If your emotional level is too high, go for therapy . . . and soon.
5. Your friends and/or family advise you to go for help and this isn't the first time they've done so.

Clues On How To Find A Therapist

Finding and choosing a therapist can be a confusing business. Perhaps these few suggestions will serve to make your search for the right therapist for you a little easier.

1. Get names from your local clergyperson, doctor, or other community or school resources.
2. Consider a therapist who has helped someone you know. Don't be afraid to inquire about his/her strengths or weaknesses.
3. Shop around for references as well as names. The people mentioned in number 1 will often know the strengths and areas of special competency in the therapists whom they recommend.
4. Consult one of the centers found in the Appendix and ask for a referral if that center cannot help you directly.

What To Do At Your First Meeting

At your first meeting, be as honest and open as you can. It's your dime (more like your $50 to $125) so don't play games. By the way, some centers and even individuals have a sliding fee scale to allow for those who may not be able to pay the full fee. Don't hesitate to ask about this.

Prepare yourself by considering why you're going and what you want or expect to happen. Be as honest with yourself as you can be. If you are confused, reluctant, or in pain, tell the therapist right away.

If you feel reasonably comfortable with the therapist, stick with him/her for several visits (6 - 8) and then make a decision whether or not to continue on a long term basis.

If, on the other hand, you feel ill at ease with the therapist, ask yourself if this is only an initial reaction to therapy. But if the feeling or intuition persists for several sessions, why not discuss it with the therapist and also with someone who knows you well. You are going to be revealing a lot about yourself in order to be helped and healed, so make sure you are relatively comfortable with the therapist. If not, find out why not.

A Two Pronged Approach

Help can be received by going to therapy. It may also be gotten from going to a support group. The two are often very valuable allies in recovering. Robin Morrison in her book <u>Women Who Love Too Much</u>7 says that when she is dealing with someone who is a co-addict, she won't see that person for counseling unless she is also in a support group. The group is where she will be able to talk with people with the same type of problems. Robin has found in her professional practice that therapy alone doesn't usually work. Rarely does a person come out of co-addiction by just going to her as a counselor. When that person goes to her and also attends a support group, then growth and healing take place. Let's talk about what such groups can do for you.

Support Groups

A support group is made up of a number of people who share their burdens and victories, their failures as well as their successes. Support groups give just that: lots and lots of support. A frequently heard comment from a member of the group is: "It's so very freeing to realize that I'm not alone in facing this particular problem. Other people have gone through this experience and with varying degrees of success. Some have been very successful in doing it and that really helps because it gives me hope. Others are still striving and that helps me even more."

Another important dimension of a support group involves reaching out to help others, enabling them to think about their problems and to become aware of their needs and praying for and with them. This second dimension is a great corrective to an excessive preoccupation with self and to an extreme self-reference.

You don't have to be able to explain the exact dynamic of group support, just be willing to try it. Misery loves company, right? Well, healing and recovery do also; and they usually, if not always, take place with and in company.

People who have a problem similar to ours but who are farther along in their recovery give us hope and help to sustain our efforts. People who are worse off than we are often encourage us to give thanks to God for what we have. They also challenge us to support them by our prayers and concern. They encourage us by their determination to get well so that we too become even more determined to get well and to take the necessary steps to do so.

The Twelfth Step of AA urges members to take the actions of love and not to wait for feelings to lead. People in twelve-step programs are aware of the power of the will to set the direction for their lives. Once the will has acted, they know from experience that feelings will come along and bring themselves into conformity, but not without pain. There it is again. That phrase will be with us a great deal. Believe me, the pain is definitely worth it. As they say, the gain is worth the pain.

The Catholic diocese of Trenton, New Jersey, had a special Awareness Sunday on September 14, 1986, to help educate parishoners to the needs of the divorced. In the statement explaining what was intended, one section dealt with support groups.

"The basic vehicle for reaching out to the divorced is the support group in which hurting men and women meet weekly or monthly to share their stories and find friendship. Research now shows that people who belong to support groups work through the multiple adjustments following divorce more surely, with fewer setbacks, and are much less likely to become involved in a rebound marriage. These communities of the divorced buy their members the time they need to work through their adjustment in an atmosphere of acceptance and trust, and facilitate their re-entry into the larger Church community. Support groups also provide shaken Catholics with a new, positive experience of Church."

They again realize that the "Church" still loves them and wants to minister to them in their time of crisis.

We conclude this chapter with a series of affirmations, meditations, and exercises to keep us in shape. Use as many or as few as you like.

Enjoy yourself! That's a fine way to love and accept yourself.

Affirmations

I am a child of God. Therefore, I love myself unconditionally as God loves me.

I am responsible for my own life, and I am going to make some decisions about improving my life.

I am responsible for my own happiness, and I am going to make some decisions about being happier in my life; and

I am going to take steps right now.

Prayer

In the name of Jesus Christ, my Lord and Savior, and by the power of his precious Body and Blood I dedicate myself to him and to his service, and I take authority over all evil spirits within me or influencing me. I command them to go to Jesus. He alone is Lord and Savior.

I ask you, Lord Jesus, to give me the Holy Spirit in a new and deeper way so that I may know the truth, live the truth, and speak the truth to myself and others.

Holy Spirit, show me the way you want me to go. Teach me all over how I am to think and speak. Re-train my thought patterns and my heart patterns and all the other patterns of my life which have clouded my vision and my understanding of myself. Show me once again how

I am the dearly beloved child of my God and Father;

I am the beloved sister (brother) of Jesus;

I am your temple, your dwelling place.

A Meditation On The Twelve Spiritual Push-Ups

So many people remarked about how helpful these spiritual push-ups were that we decided to repeat them and add a short meditative comment after each of them.

1. You are my God, Father, Son, and Holy Spirit, in whom I place my trust. (You have been a faithful God and I thank you for always caring and providing for me and mine. Your track record in caring for me helps me to trust you even more for today and all days.)

2. Your presence, my God, is everywhere. (You are here with me now and you are everywhere I will ever go. If I forget

you, I know you'll never forget or leave me alone.)

3. Your presence surrounds me. In you, I live and move and have my being. (Let me never forget how close you are to me and how close I am to you. Let me learn to live, move, and have my being in a conscious affirmation of you as the source of all my strength and holiness.)

4. Your presence is within me, strengthening, inspiring, healing, and perfecting me. (Thank you for making me your dwelling place, your temple of flesh and blood. Help me to accept your strength, your inspiration, and your healing. Don't let me forget that perfection is your gift and not the first of your gifts either.)

5. The presence of your Holy Spirit drives out fear and worry and anxiety. (Do it, Lord God, and I give you my permission to work in the deep recesses of my being to free me from not trusting you.)

6. The presence of your Holy Spirit gives me strength for all my needs. (Here are my needs for the day as I see them. I'm listing the main ones, but also giving you carte blanche to do what is best for me.)

7. The presence of your Holy Spirit banishes resentment and hatred and subdues anger. (How those feelings of resentment and hatred persist in my life. Help me to eradicate them at their source. Enter into areas of my anger to calm and guide me so that I may learn how to be angry and not to sin.

9. The inspiration of your Holy Spirit

gives me understanding so that I may have clearness of vision, steadfastness of thought, and trueness of speech. (Lord, I need to discover, understand, and articulate a vision for my life. Enlighten my mind and touch my eyes that I may see you. Cleanse my lips that I may speak the truth in love to you, myself, and others.)

10. The presence of your Holy Spirit enables me to overcome disease and evil in all forms. (O God of loveliness and might, free me from all forms of evil and guide me on the everlasting way. Hide me in your holiness and protect me. Do more by making me victorious over evil and all kinds of disease.)

11. Nothing and no one can separate me from your Holy Spirit. (Only I can do that and today I once again choose to be chosen by you. Lord, I repeat and reaffirm my 'yes' to being your disciple and your friend.)

12. Praise to you, o Lord, who gives me victory through Jesus Christ, my Savior, in the power of the Holy Spirit. (Let me learn the joy of praising you for being you: one God and three persons ever to be adored and loved.)

An Exercise

Lie on the floor or a bed and get comfortable, but not too comfortable. Breathe deeply from your abdomen. Do this a few times and then say the following.

I *have* a *body*. Breathe in the love of

the Lord as you say the words and then breathe out pain and hurt from all the parts of your body. Breathe in the love of Jesus and feel him touch the areas of your body which need his healing love. When you feel at ease physically, conclude this section by saying, "Yes, I have a body and it is God's gift to me. But I am not just my body. I am more than a body."

Now say, <u>I have a mind</u>. Bring some thought which occupied you during the day or night back into your consciousness. Think it again and then ask Jesus to come into your thought processes and show you if the thought were true or false. Ask for wisdom in this particular matter. Then conclude with the words, "Yes, I have a mind and thoughts. But I am not just a mind or thoughts. I am more than my mind and my thoughts."

Next say, <u>I have emotions</u>. Then think about one emotion which was very powerful in the last few days. Feel it again with all its force. Then ask the Lord to help you feel the opposite emotion. If you have been happy, feel sadness. If you have felt rejected, feel acceptance. If you have felt anger at another person, feel compassion toward that other.

Take the time to feel both sides of the emotion. Conclude by saying, "Yes, I have emotions. But I am not just my emotions. I am more than my emotions."

Finally say, "Thank you, Jesus, for giving me a body to act with, a mind to think with, and emotions with which to feel. Free me from a one-dimensional approach to these areas of my life. Thank you for all these dimensions of who I am, and help me to realize that I am unique and inexpressibly beautiful as you have made me. I am more than a body, a mind, and emotions. I one day can live with you forever. Thank you for this vocation to be yours and thank you for the grace to live out my vocation."

How To Pray For Healing With Another

Every baptized Christian is called to be on Jesus' healing team.8 We often teach people how to pray for healing. First of all we ask them to put their hand on the person with whom they are praying, but not to say anything. People are always so anxious that they will not say the right word. By simply touching the person and letting God's love flow into and through us to the other, we let God do what he wants to do. We open our hearts and let the language of heaven be the only one spoken.9

Use The Language Of Love!

What is the language of heaven? Love. And so when we pray with love we do not have to say anything, but just open ourselves to the love of God. We drink it in and then let it flow out to the one for whom we are praying. No human language or verbalization can ever compare with the love we show. The prayer is done under the power of the Holy Spirit. It begins with Jesus, continues with him, and by him is brought to completion.

Keep your eyes on him. Have you ever noticed how traffic slows down when there is an accident or construction ahead? Drivers take their eyes off the road and stare at what's happening. Thank God they do slow down. Each of us has probably done the same thing ourselves.

In praying for healing, don't take your eyes off Jesus and focus on something or someone else. Lots of things can clutter our minds and hearts: am I saying the "right" words? is this the "proper" way to pray? how are the "others" doing it? Gently dismiss these distractions from your mind and heart, and once again as always try to focus all your attention on Jesus.

Responsibility

The following reflections may interest you. They may inspire you, infuriate you, or affect you in some other way. Enjoy them. Like them. Or hate them. Accept them. Or change them.

I am responsible
    for what I say
    for what I am
    for what I feel
    for what I do
I am <u>not</u> responsible
    for making anyone else happy

>   for becoming what someone else wants me to be
>   for telling an untruth to keep from hurting another's feelings

I am responsible
>   when someone breaks a secret I told them because I was a poor judge of character
>   when people use what I say to hurt me because I should be able to tell when a person does not wish me well
>   for defending myself
>   for the ties other people have with me because it takes two to tango
>   for everything in my life that would not be there unless I did something

If I don't like my lifestyle,
> I am responsible.

If I don't like my job,
> I am responsible.

If I don't like my home,
> I am responsible.

If I don't like my spouse,
> I am responsible.

If I don't like the way I am treated,
> I am responsible.

If I don't like me,
> I am responsible.

I am responsible for <u>everything</u> in my life, all the successes and failures. Without taking responsibility for my life, I will never be happy because no one can fix my life but <u>me</u>. Without taking responsibility for my life, no risk is worth taking, since I will not feel joy at my success and living becomes merely an exercise in wishful thinking.

Anonymous

FOOTNOTES

1. <u>Centerlines</u> (Center for Human Development), no. 4 (1981), p. 15.
2. Ibid., p. 14.
3. Gerald P. Ruane, <u>Birth to Birth</u> (New York: Alba House, 1976), pp. 35-36.
4. Waltrased Herbstrith, <u>Edith Stein, A Biography</u>, pp. 112-113.
5. David Roper in "The Idaho Statesman," Boise, Idaho, Sunday, July 12, 1976.
6. Warren Molton, "Friends, Partners and Lovers" on <u>Two Become One</u>, cassette (Kansas City, Missouri: National Catholic Reporter Publishing Co., 1977).
7. Robin Morrison, <u>Women Who Love Too Much</u> (New York: Pocket Books, 1985), p.224.
8. Gerald P. Ruane, <u>Overcoming Obstacles to Healing</u> (Caldwell, New Jersey: Sacred Heart Press, 1985), pp. 10-15.
9. A speaker once told a group of us priests to be very respectful of the Polish because Polish is the language of heaven. This was even a few years before our Polish pope came on the scene. We all laughed, but I must admit that I did go out and learn a few phrases in Polish just in case I needed them to get me through the gates of heaven.

FIRST SECTION

Introduction

In our first section we consider two emotions which are often serious obstacles to healing: fear and unresolved anger. There's a presupposition that both of them are negative and to be avoided. Actually, that's not completely true. Both of these emotions involve tremendous energy which can be used either constructively or destructively.

The formula which we have found helpful is three-fold: recognize the emotion, face it, and then handle it in the most appropriate way. When either of these emotions is used destructively, then we really do need the healing power of the Lord to help us identify its cause and to give us the wisdom to know what the proper remedies are.

Fear not, for I have redeemed you;
    I have called you by name; you are mine.
When you pass through the water, I will be with you
    in the rivers you shall not drown.
When you walk through fire, you shall not be burned;
    the flames shall not consume you.
                              Isaiah 43

CHAPTER II

FREEDOM FROM FEARS THROUGH FAITH WHICH FOCUSES ON JESUS

"Do not live in fear, little flock. It has pleased your Father to give you the kingdom." (Lk 12:32)

"This was the oath he swore to our father Abraham: to set us <u>free from</u> the hands of our enemies; <u>free to</u> worship him without fear."(Lk 1:73-74)

Zechariah's canticle from the Gospel according to St. Luke is a powerful statement of God's plan to free his people from their fears. Our translation stresses this reality.

> Blessed be the Lord, the God of Israel.
> He has come to his people and set them <u>free</u>.
> He has raised up for us a mighty <u>liberator</u>,
> born of the house of his servant David.
>
> Through his holy prophets he promised of old
> that he would <u>free us from</u> our enemies
> from the hands of all who hate us.
> He promised to show mercy to our fathers

and to remember his holy covenant.
This was the oath he swore to our
   father Abraham:
to set us <u>free from</u> the hands of our
   enemies,
free to worship him without fear, holy
   and righteous in his sight all the
   days of our lives.

You, my child, shall be called the
   prophet of the Most High,
for you will go before the Lord to
   prepare his way,
to give his people knowledge of salvation by
<u>freeing</u> <u>them</u> <u>from</u> <u>their</u> <u>sins</u>.

In the <u>tender</u> <u>compassion</u> of our God,
the dawn from on high shall break upon
   us,
to <u>free</u> those who dwell in darkness
   and the shadow of death,
and to guide our feet into the way of
   peace. (Lk 1:67-79)

    God wants to <u>free</u> <u>us</u> <u>from</u> fears and anxieties so that he can <u>free</u> <u>us</u> <u>to</u> worship him without fear and to live life to the full as he desires. The result of his liberating action in our lives is that we may have peace and may walk confidently in the way of peace.
    Fears and anxieties grip us all peri- odically and can be very helpful at times. There are certain things and people we should fear. In their presence, we need the

extra physical and emotional strength a healthy fear can provide to respond to "the enemy."

A distinction may be helpful. A person can act "from fear" or "with fear." "From fear" means he does something because of fear. A shotgun wedding used to be the obvious case of such fear. A man has defiled a woman and her family forces him at gun point or by some other means to marry her. The wedding would never have taken place if the fear had not been present. Fear destroyed the freedom that had to be there for a valid marriage contract.

On the other hand, almost every wedding takes place "with fear" to some extent. A bride and groom often have hidden fears about being good spouses, lovers, friends, and partners to the other. Normally such fears do not destroy or significantly weaken their consent to the marriage. Each of them decides to put the fears in perspective and make an act of faith in self, the other partner, and in God who is the bond between them.

Cancer of the Spirit

"Cancer of the spirit" is the way one doctor described fear. This doctor, herself a cancer specialist, is constantly frustrated by people who put off seeing her for months and even years. Yes, such people worry about their symptoms, but they are more afraid of knowing what is going on in their bodies. Fear prevents them from getting up the courage to do anything about their condition. By the time they overcome their fear and finally get to a doctor, the situation is often critical. Fears of illness, of doctors, or of the worst possible diagnosis are very common but also very costly fears.

Medical professionals are rightfully frustrated and angry when people refuse to use their services until it's too late. Such fears are common among adults. Others are more prevalent among children and would be amusing if they weren't so real to the child.

A nurse told me how she learned to handle a child's fear of needles. Children think that their bodies are like balloons, and they fear that if they are punctured by a needle all the air will come out of their bodies. As a pediatric nurse, she learned very quickly to reassure the child that putting a bandage over the needle mark would make everything all right. She felt that it was better to face and ease the child's fear, unfounded in reality but very real to the child. Only after that could the child be helped to understand what the body was truly like. That's a very good approach to fear in yourself and others.

A three-step approach to fear has been helpful for many people. First, recognize the fear. Own it. It's yours. Second, face it. Speak to it and ask: what or who are you? And third, handle it, but not alone. Get the help you need from the Lord, from

professionals, if necessary, and from other people.
When our fears get "out of control," we have a phobia. A phobia generates uncontrollable panic when there is no real danger. We'll discuss phobias at the end of this chapter.

Give Fear A Proper Name

People suffer from a wide variety of fears, including the fear of:
> flying and sailing
> spiders and snakes
> bad dreams
> high places
> the dark and shadows
> elevators and closed-in places
> large crowds and strangers.

The list seems endless as there is a veritable alphabet of fears which plague us.
Some fears which are great obstacles to healing are:
1. fear of rejection, of losing significance and worth;
2. fear of poverty, illness, and being alone; of losing control of our lives;
3. fear of God because he may not be able to help me or, if he does, the gain won't be worth the pain;
4. fear of eternal damnation, of slipping out of God's grace at the last moment.[1]
Recently someone gave me a picture of Jesus as a young man with red hair and a very red beard, red eyebrows, and very dark

luminous brown eyes, almost reddish. (I must admit, a red-haired Jesus made me sit up and take notice!) At the bottom of the painting were the words: "Christ, the essence of light, life, love and laughter." The thesis of this chapter is that our fears, whatever they are, and no matter how many or few they are, will only be faced if we have Christ with us. He truly is the essence of light, life, love, and laughter. That fourth characteristic of Jesus, laughter, is not to be despised.

Focusing On Jesus

Freedom from fears comes by focusing on Jesus, but not in a one-dimensional, tunnel-visioned way. Freedom from fears comes in many ways and usually in a gradual process.

Here are some Scripture passages which may help. In your quiet time with the Lord, which is a most important element in the healing of our fears, why not take one of these passages as your starting point?

All of Psalm 27, but especially verses 1 and 3: The Lord is my light and my salvation, whom should I fear? The Lord is my life's refuge, of whom should I be afraid? . . . Though an army encamp against me, my heart will not fear; though war be waged upon me, even then will I trust.

Isaiah 42, especially verses 1b and 5a: Fear not for I have redeemed you; I have called you by name; you are mine . . . Fear not for I am with you.

Jesus wants to cast out all fear and he tells us that in John 14:1 when he says: "Do not let your hearts be troubled."

You might also use the following which I can only hope you will find beneficial on your healing journey.

Your Heavenly Father Knows And Provides

"I warn you, then: do not worry about your livelihood, what you are to eat or drink or use for clothing. Is not life more than food? Is not the body more valuable than clothes?

"Look at the birds in the sky. They do not sow or reap, they gather nothing into barns; yet your heavenly Father feeds them. Are you not more important than they? Which of you by worrying can add a moment to his life-span? As for clothes, why be concerned? Learn a lesson from the way the wild flowers grow. They do not work; they do not spin. Yet I assure you, not even Solomon in all his splendor was arrayed like one of these. If God can clothe in such splendor the grass of the field which blooms today and is thrown on the fire tomorrow, will he not provide much more for you, o weak in faith! Stop worrying then over questions like, 'What are we to eat, or what are we to drink, or what are we to wear?' The unbelievers are always running after these things. Your heavenly Father knows all that you need. Seek first his kingship over you, his way of holiness, and all these things will be given you besides. Enough, then, of worrying about tomorrow. Let tomorrow take care of itself. Today has troubles enough of its own." (Mt 6:25-34)

Do Not Be Afraid!

Immediately afterward, while dismissing the crowds, Jesus insisted that his disciples get into the boat and precede him to the other side. When he had sent them away, he went up on the mountain by himself to pray, remaining there as evening drew on. Meanwhile, the boat, already several hundred yards out from shore, was being tossed about in the waves raised by strong headwinds. At about three in the morning, he came walking towards them on the lake. When the disciples saw him walking on the water, they were terrified."It is a ghost!" they said, and in their fear they began to cry out. Jesus hastened to reassure them: "Get hold of yourselves! It is I. Do not be afraid!" Peter spoke up and said, "Lord, if it is really you, tell me to come to you across the water."

"Come!" he said. So Peter got out of the boat and began to walk on the water, moving toward Jesus. But when he perceived how strong the wind was, becoming frightened, he began to sink and cried out, "Lord, save me!" Jesus at once stretched out his hand and caught him. "How little faith you have!" he exclaimed. "Why did you falter?" Once they had climbed into the boat, the wind died down. (Mt 14:22-33)

Children of God

All who are led by the Spirit of God are children of God. You did not receive a spirit of slavery leading you back into fear, but a spirit of adoption, through which we cry out, "Abba!" (that is, "Father"). The Spirit himself gives witness with our spirit that we are children of God. But if we are children, we are heirs as well: heirs of God, heirs with Christ, if only we suffer with him so as to be glorified with him. (Rom 8:14-17)

The Spirit God has given us is no cowardly spirit, but rather one that makes us strong, loving, and wise. Therefore, never be ashamed of your testimony to our Lord, nor of me, a prisoner for his sake; but with the strength which comes from God bear your share of hardship which the Gospel entails. (2 Tim 1:7-8)

Perfect Love Casts Out All Fear

Our love is brought to perfection in this, that we should have <u>confidence</u> on the day of judgment; for our relation to this world is just like his. Love has no room for fear; rather, perfect love casts out all fear. And since fear has to do with punishment, love is not yet perfect in one who is afraid. We, for our part, love because he first loved us.

If you use a journal to record your

thoughts and feelings each day, you may want to list your fears. In your daily prayer time, take one fear and pray about it. Then, write a letter to Jesus about your fear and what you hope to do about it. Stay close to the Lord and with him as your companion face your fear as it manifests itself.

A Group Helps

In a small sharing group a very lively woman - physically, spiritually, and mentally - mentioned how the Lord had revealed to her in some dreams that she was afraid of dying. Working as a hospice volunteer was something that she enjoyed but it was harming her personal life. Several members of her family had died of cancer, and she feared that she would also. The other people in the group offered some interesting advice on how to handle her fear.

One person mentioned that when he is afraid he just commands the fear to leave, saying it has no place there. He belongs to Jesus, and the Lord's perfect love casts out fear. His faith helps him overcome fear. Since he had a heart attack about ten years ago, he had come to realize that this was the way to handle some of his fears about sickness and death.

Another woman in the group remarked: "I see in you a little child - the inner child - who is very fearful. Why not let the adult part of you have a talk with that inner child and try to reassure, affirm, and love her?"

The group also agreed that a very good response to her fear was to begin thanking God for the vibrant health that she was obviously enjoying at that time. An attitude of gratitude seemed a good remedy for much of what she was experiencing.

Only With Jesus

My own experience has shown me the need to face my fears, but not alone. I try to do so with Jesus and let him guide me. One instance, not terribly earth-shaking in itself, did, however, teach me a very valuable lesson. Once, while giving a day of recollection, as I was being introduced I suddenly imagined myself walking to the podium and falling flat on my face. Naturally I put that out of my mind with the comment, "I'm too suave to do anything quite like that." But then the Lord said, "Get serious, and walk through that scene. Don't push it down, don't ignore it. Face it." So I did.

I pictured myself walking up to the podium and falling flat on my face. I also pictured what would happen. The leaders' group had prayed with me for twenty minutes previously and I was deeply touched by their concern for me. I imagined that the leaders and others too would rush to pick me up, brush me off, and get me a drink of water. They would pray with me, anoint me, and get me ready to give my talk. In reality, I probably would have gotten a lot more prayer and done a better job if it had happened. By the way, it didn't happen except in my imagination; but it taught me a lot about fear.

Facing our fears with Jesus is the answer. But do you realize how many people fear God and his intentions for them? They fear they may have to change, and do not know if they can do so. They are afraid to leave their present unhappiness to move into the unknown. What seems to happen is that a two-fold fear seizes them. They are afraid of the known but even more afraid of the unknown. "The devil you know is better than the devil you don't know" isn't good theology, nor was it ever very good advice.

A Christ-Centered Approach

Our faith in God must confront our fear of him and the future. It's only as we focus on God's love made flesh in Jesus Christ that we can face the future with confidence. When we stop and look at our thinking along these lines, we can see that it is foolish to keep God at arm's length. God is truly our Prodigal Father who makes Jesus the Way for us. Ours is admittedly a very Christ-centered approach, but is there any other one capable of so quickly leading us from fear to faith-filled confidence?

The hymn "Lord Jesus, Once You Spoke To Men" has a beautiful second verse:

> We all have hidden fears to face
> Our minds and motives to amend;

> We seek your truth, we need your grace
> Our living Lord and present Friend.

Those last two lines say it all. We can face our hidden fear and anything else as long as we realize that Jesus, our living Lord and present Friend, is helping us.

So often we fear what God may ask us to do if he heals us. One person, bothered by a severe personal problem, sought healing; but always held back a part of himself. Why? He secretly believed he'd have to become a priest if he were healed. Although he was repeatedly told that God wasn't demanding that commitment of him, he could not shake the fear. His fear had no rational foundation; but then, fear isn't reasonable. It's just there, and it needs to be addressed. The young man eventually was healed of his fear which, of course, cleared the way for further healing.

Death And Dying

Fear of death and dying is a very common fear. For many years I studied about death and also taught a college course entitled "The Meaning of Death, Suffering, and Healing." In some quarters my nickname was "The Death Theologian," which I hope referred more to the topic than to the presentation. Once I was asked by a radio interviewer, "You're not afraid of death anymore, are you?" I replied immediately, "Yes! I am afraid, if not of death then of dying. I am not as afraid as I was before studying, writing, and teaching about the subject; but I'm still afraid to some degree."

In a section of a previous book, <u>Birth to Birth: the Life-Death Mystery</u>, I attempted to explain why and how we fear dying. I made a distinction between a child's fear and that of an adult. Published in 1976, the book was an attempt to explain this topic in a succinct way and to help the reader to begin reflecting on his or her own fears.

Fear And The Dying

"Fear can be a constant companion of those who are sick or dying. Fear has many disguises - the fear of the unknown, the fear of being alone and the fear of pain which intensifies our sufferings.

"We humans are beset by so many fears, and they seem to surface most forcefully when we are seriously ill or suspect that we are dying.

"It is important to realize that fear will be there at such times and to understand why it is there and what, if anything, can be done about it.

"No matter how old we are, part of us is still a child. A child's fear feeds on the minor discomforts and inconveniences of normal patient care. A child's fear must be seen for what it is and efforts made to ease it. The patient experiencing such fear must be soothed and reassured as we would do with any worried or frightened child.

"An adult fear arises when the ultimate questions are faced. What is death? What will it mean for me and for my loved ones? What comes after death? Reading about such things now, reflecting upon them and confronting their implications will modify and lessen that type of fear.

"Nothing will remove our fears completely. <u>Someone</u> might. And to many of us, that someone is our loving God and Father who is stronger than fear, stronger than death itself.

"<u>Side Street</u>: (Wander down it and enjoy the scenery and diversion. Come back to the main road when you are ready.)

"Fear has been compared to another person living within us who will always have the upper hand unless we tear away his mask of anonymity.

"Fear faced in faith is fear weakened.

"Fear faced with Jesus is fear conquered."[2]

In the eleven years since I wrote that excerpt I have faced and conquered some fears with the help of Jesus. Other fears linger on, but not so strongly as before. With them, I'm still in the process, but getting better at it.

What helped me overcome my fear were the theories of some great theologians, but most of all the stories of some equally great non-theologians. For instance, one Felician sister from Chicago has made a banner with the words:

In grief, let us put our arms around each other.

In joy, let us sing and dance together.

In life, let us celebrate our health.

In death, let us celebrate our hope.

That pretty well sums up a good plan to live fully and die happily.

Death As Mercy

Death is not the ultimate enemy. Sometimes it is the loving response of God to our pleas. "That's enough, Lord, please, take me home." Death is occasionally called the ultimate healing. Don't believe it. Death is the last stop on the way to ultimate healing, which is the resurrection. We are made to live forever with Christ, our risen Lord, who died and rose from the dead to give us courage to face death and see it for what it is.

Death is the doorway we gently push aside as we enter into the life of our God who is Father, Son, and Holy Spirit.

Recently the aging and aged have come into their own through the Gray Panthers and Gray Power movements. Yet in our "youth crazed and fixated culture" there is in many of us a real fear of the aging process and all that it seems to bring.

The fear of getting older with its concommitant decrease in our freedom, mobility, and health can be conquered by humor and by the help of friends. The next two poems highlight these two approaches respectively.

Cardinal Richard Cushing, Archbishop of Boston for many years, once reflected how all too quickly his life was passing by. He wrote a poem on the shape in which he found himself in his declining years.

I'm Fine

I live out in Brighton close to BC (Boston College)
And I'm just as healthy as I can be,
I have arthritis in both my knees
And when I must speak, then I talk with a wheeze.
My pulse is weak and my blood is quite thin,
But I'm awfully well for the shape that I'm in.

I need arch supporters to strengthen my feet,
My ankles are swollen; I'm white as a sheet,
I toss in my bed without sleep every night,
No wonder each morning I look such a sight.
My memory is failing, my head's in a spin,
But I'm awfully well for the shape that I'm in.

Diverticulitis is a word hard to spell,
But it's a disease from which I'll never get well.
Ulcers that keep me on a diet with Maalox
Prevent me from resting in a funeral box.
The length of my sermons brings yawns or a grin,
But I'm awfully well for the shape that I'm in.

The moral is, friends, as this tale I unfold,
That for you and for me who are fast growing old
It's better to say, "I'm fine," with a grin
Than to let people know of the shape that we're in.

Despite his moral, the good Cardinal spent most of the poem telling us the shape that he was in; but he did it with humor and a grin and a few good pokes at his own behavior. He lived until he died, and he did it very well. That's a worthy goal for all of us.

The next poem would have been much more depressing except for the contemporaries who shared dreams and reality with the old man of the sea, born to sail and sail again.

Born To Sail Again

Through the thundering swells of churning ocean
    glided a vessel of strength.
    And its captain stood on the bow with the pride
    of his abilities and a feeling of worthiness.
    Never did he forsee the toll that this ocean of unpredictability
    would take on him.
    He was an old man of the sea, born to sail again.

    With his ship tattered and unable to keep afloat,
    The old man sat on the docks with his head hung
    in helplessness and despair.
    The sea of life had indeed shook its fist at him
    without mercy.
    He was an old man of the sea, born to sail again.

    Day after day he sat and dreamed of the times
    at sea he once had.
    Times of feeling: feeling the ocean spray against his face.
    How he longed for those times again.
    And so it happened that a group of older men came upon him,
    And they shared with him their own tragedies with the sea.

And together they mended each of their ships.
He was an old man of the sea, born to sail again.

With each of their dream vessels repaired,
They challenged the toll of the sea together;
Each able to reinforce the other when the high seas were rough.
And the old man of the sea sailed once again.3

Don't Worry About Tomorrow!

Often what we fear does not happen. Many, many times we waste tremendous psychic energy in worrying and being anxious about things that never happen. A very helpful poster proclaims:

Don't worry about tomorrow!
You did that yesterday.

I have added another line:

And it didn't do you any good.

Think about those sentiments. You may want to change my words in the third line to fit your own needs. Be my guest.
Even when you have faced your fears there may be a remnant or residue left in your mind and heart. When you become aware of that residue, try thanking God for the

gift of life and all the blessings in your life. Please understand how powerful and healing an attitude of gratitude can be.

All our fears can be faced if we are secure enough in God's love. When we stand encircled by his love and truth, we truly are rooted and grounded in one whose strength is greater by far than ours. And that strength is ours for the asking.

Once while on an eight-day directed retreat the first scripture passage I was given to meditate upon spoke about Joseph, the husband of Mary and Protector of the Child Jesus. I stayed with that passage for a long time and, in the process, became acquainted in very personal ways with Joseph the Obedient, the Do-er, the Strong One, the manly husband and foster father. Joseph was certainly not given to many words (none are recorded in the Gospels). Joseph was the original "yes man" and in the best sense of that phrase. He deserves to be hailed as Joseph the Obedient.

As the days of the retreat went on, my meditation expanded to include Mary and Jesus. I felt absorbed into the Holy Family. The conviction grew within me that I had a charter membership in the Holy Family. They wanted me and I wanted that great privilege. It was a beautiful experience. I used my imagination, my writings, and very simple drawings to picture myself with Jesus, Mary, and Joseph. Fears of rejection and poverty and of sickness which had been bothering me for years began to fade in the warmth of their love. Perhaps you will feel a similar call to membership in the Holy Family. If so, rejoice in that fact and enjoy it as much as you can.

The bumper sticker on a car proclaimed: "God is my Father. Jesus is my Brother. The Spirit dwells within me. Mary is my Mother. Don't you think I have a very Holy Family?" That's a lot to get on a bumper sticker, but it's all true. Believe it. Repeat it often. Proclaim it to yourself and others.

Rooted and grounded in the love of Father, Son, and Holy Spirit, and welcomed into the Holy Family of Jesus, Mary, and Joseph, you will be able to face your fears and bring them out of their hiding places into the light.

The value of a spiritual friend has been stressed by many authors, but here it has even greater importance. Telling one's fears to a friend helps immensely. A friend may also be able to remind you of certain resources and devotional aids which you have been too emotionally disturbed to remember.

Thomas Merton, one of the greatest religious thinkers and writers of our times, had to face some very dark moments in his own personal spiritual journey.

"My Lord God, I have no idea where I am going. I do not see the road ahead of me. I cannot know for certain where it will end. Nor do I really know myself, and the fact that I think that I am following your

will does not mean that I am actually doing so. But I believe that the desire to please you does, in fact, please you. And I hope I have that desire in all that I am doing. I hope that I will never do anything apart from that desire. And I know that if I do this, you will lead me by the right road though I may know nothing about it. Therefore, I will trust you always though I may seem to be lost and in the shadow of death. I will not fear, for you are ever with me, and you will never leave me to face my perils alone.
    Thomas Merton"

   Our Institute newsletter carried the following words of St. Francis de Sales, and many people expressed their appreciation.

Do Not Fear

what may happen tomorrow.
The same loving Father
who cares for you today
will care for you tomorrow
and every day.

Either he will shield you
from suffering
or he will give you
unfailing strength
to bear it.

Be at peace, then,
and put aside all

anxious thoughts
and imaginings.

When I was going through some rough times personally and not handling the combination of fear and stress too well, a friend reminded me of St. Francis de Sales' prayer. The words helped and she helped very much by her affectionate concern as she reached out to remind me of some very important truths.

Phobias And Healing

Just a few words on the topic of phobias may be helpful. Phobias are "fears out of control" and usually require professional help. A partial listing of phobias follows and may help in more ways than simply vocabulary building. "Phobia" is Greek for "fear." The first part of the name refers to the object of the fear.

> Aerophobia: flying
> Agoraphobia: marketplace
> Amaxophobia: vehicles, driving
> Anthropophobia: people
> Aquaphobia: water
> Claustrophobia: closed spaces
> Cynophobia: dogs
> Gephyrophobia: bridges
> Nyctophobia: darkness
> Ochlophobia: crowds
> Ophidiophobia: snakes
> Panophobia: everything
> Phobophobia: fear of fears

    Phonophobia: speaking aloud
    Pyrophobia: fire
    Thanatophobia: death
    Xenophobia: strangers

While a phobia may often begin in a limited way, it can become the dominant concern of the person who may then resort to extreme measures of self-protection. A cab driver who developed a terror of driving began handcuffing himself to his steering wheel so that he could make a living and support his family.

Typical phobic symptoms are much like the symptoms of a heart attack so people experiencing their first phobic attack often end up in the hospital. After the initial attack, a phobic tries to avoid situations which will trigger a reaction.

Most therapists encourage their phobic patients to confront their fears in real-life situations. By enduring a feared situation for fifteen to twenty seconds, the phobic realizes that the panic will often subside as he or she learns to distract thoughts of panic by doing such things as praying, telephoning a friend, talking out loud, or whatever. Phobics also recover when a sympathetic person, often a recovered phobic, helps them get through the panic.

A typical treatment program consists of two related segments. A phobic meets privately with a mental health professional and then joins a group counseling session. The latter helps because it lets the patient know he is not the only person with this terrible affliction, and that others are willing to help him face his fears because they need his help to face their own.

The next step is called desensitization, during which the person begins to work up courage to confront his or her fear. Someone who was afraid of riding in elevators sought help. At first she and her counselor just looked into an elevator; then a week later they stepped inside. After five weeks they rode up a floor together. At the end of two months, the woman took her first solo ride in an elevator in many years.

Two things which help the healing process are the <u>desire</u> of the person to overcome the fear and the <u>amount of effort</u> he puts into it. Some phobics fail to recover because either they refuse to or are afraid to confront their fears.

Contemporary phobia theory has transformed this once virtually incurable mental illness into one which can be quickly and reliably treated. Too few people know that help is available. God wants us to use all available means to be healed if such means do not conflict with his law and good common sense.

If you are bothered by phobias, I urge you to seek professional help. You might begin by sending a self-addressed, stamped envelope to the Phobia Society of America, 6191 Executive Boulevard, Rockville, Maryland 20852. This group has done a great deal to help thousands of people who suffer from phobic reactions. More and more is being written about phobias, even in more popular magazines. The Reader's Digest, for instance, carried an excellent article on this topic in the August 1984 issue. Titled "How Phobias Can Be Healed," the article has helped me in my work and writing and I recommend it highly.

Concluding Prayer

Lord, I'm afraid of so many things, but I believe that you are the good shepherd and you will never abandon me. You continually tell me, "Walk with me and go at my pace. Trust me to take you to the next stage of growth. Walk with me and stay by my side. Don't go off on your own."
Lord, I don't want to lose you. Help me to heed and follow your words.
Thank you for helping me face my hidden fears, for giving me your grace and truth. You really are my living Lord and my ever-present Friend.

FOOTNOTES

1. The incorrect ambush theory of God promoted this fear when we were told that God was just waiting for us to make one false move and then he'd get us.
2. Ruane, Birth to Birth, p. 32.
3. A retired navy chaplain shared this with me. It had appeared in a newsletter out of the Great Lakes Naval Training Ctr.

Merciful and gracious is the Lord,
    slow to anger and abounding in kindness.
He will not always chide,
    nor does he keep his wrath forever.
Not according to our sins does he deal
        with us,
    nor does he requite us according to our
        crimes.

                                    Psalm 103

CHAPTER III

ANGER: POWER FOR THE KINGDOM

"If you are angry, let it be without sin. The sun must not go down on your wrath." (Eph 4:26)

Anger is not an obstacle to healing if we follow St. Paul's advice to the Ephesians. However, anger can well be an obstacle and a very dangerous one. Many people fear anger greatly. They have an unhealthy fear for what can be a positive emotion. Perhaps as children they may have exploded with a very violent reaction at someone or something. Because of the vehemence of their own reaction, or how parents or others reacted, many people often become very frightened of their own anger. They learn to suppress it, and thus never face it. Their anger remains unresolved and often develops the destructive force of a time bomb.

Other people fear their anger because they have seen how parents or significant others have used anger with great hostility. One man mentioned that he feared anger because his parents used it against each other. They would become angry, have a very hostile exchange, and not talk to one another for days. Eventually, they resumed talking but only until the next explosion. Nothing ever seemed to get resolved by his parents' anger. In fact, their hostility to each other just continued to increase. As a consequence, he began to fear his anger and to bottle it up. When it exploded, was it ever destructive! Just ask his family about it!

A Valuable Asset

Anger is a valuable natural asset. Without it, our race would probably not have survived. When our ancestors were threatened, adrenalin coursed through their bodies, preparing them to fight or flee, depending upon the nature of the threat. Anger helped them to fight off animals that threatened their children or it lent wings to their feet when a forest fire raged out of control.

While not many of us are seriously threatened today (except on the roads and streets of big towns), we are often frustrated. Frustration is another source of anger. When our needs are not met - a need for peace and quiet, for a fair employer, an understanding spouse - our frustration gives rise to anger.

Frustration plus anger can lead to aggression. We are hurting and, in turn, we feel the impulse to inflict pain. Thus a frustrated and angry motorist may be tempted to punch another driver in the nose. That could be dangerous as the other driver might be a professional boxer or have some friends nearby.

A final problem is hostility. If we fail to identify and deal with our frustrations, they will lead to hostility. We will find ourselves moving through life with a chip constantly on our shoulder waiting for some hapless spouse, child, or neighbor to knock it off.

Anger, aggression, hostility are three very different dimensions of human behavior. Anger is a useful, even valuable, emotion. Aggression and hostility clearly are not healthy ways of venting one's anger.

A Brick For Building Or Killing

Let us imagine that our anger is a brick. We have the choice of throwing it at the other person or setting it down between us as the cornerstone of a good relationship. The latter approach is the healthy and optimistic one and, of course, is the one recommended by this author.

Please note that no one is going to be perfect at this. So relax and try to avoid self-condemnation. Learn to apologize when you have used your anger inappropriately or even destructively. God doesn't expect perfection of us in this area or any other. Just keep giving him the chance to work in you and with you so that he can teach you how to be angry and sin not, and to build healthy relationships with the brick of that very positive emotion: anger.

Once again, let's say it. Anger is a powerful human emotion. As an emotion, it is not good or bad; it just is. Anger is there and we have to deal with it. Anger can be very good at times.

Anger And Some Biblical Figures

The Bible's list of angry people reads like <u>Who's Who</u>: Moses, Jesus, and Yahweh himself to name but a few. They were not angry always and everywhere, but at times they were exceedingly angry.

Moses smashed the stone tablets of the Law when he saw the golden calf!

Yahweh, our God, is said to have been stirred to anger on numerous occasions when the Israelites proved unfaithful.

And Jesus, the Lord, was himself so angry that he drove the money changers from the Temple. He was angry at injustice and at the hypocrisy of the Pharisees and even with his own disciples who were so slow to learn and so often suffered from "foot-in-mouth" disease.

Jesus is the model of being angry in a healthy and constructive way for he is the angry Christian par excellence.

The Angry Conference

The Association of Christian Therapists (A.C.T.) is an organization of medical and health care professionals and those in related areas of healing and caring who believe in the healing power of Jesus which they integrate into their own lives and practices. A.C.T. once had a five day conference on anger. It turned out to be the angriest conference I have ever attended.

The first day and a half were taken up with the theory of anger, reflecting upon anger very intellectually and safely. All of a sudden, there came a time when the anger which had been examined so dispassionately began to be felt and expressed with great force. It was as if we, the participants, had been given permission to express what had been repressed too long.

Doctors were angry at nurses and nurses were furious with doctors; priests were angry at sisters and sisters were very definitely angry at priests. Within all the medical, health care, and healing specialties, there was anger because of put-downs, lack of respect, misunderstandings, and poor communication.

Anger had been talked about, then it reared its ugly head; but it turned out to be not so ugly after all. Anger was definitely there; and, believe me, everyone felt it. When the participants admitted their anger and gave it a respectful hearing, it lost its power to harm and to hinder growth. Thank God, the meeting lasted for five days so that the anger could be faced, accepted, and resolved. Many valuable techniques for integrating anger into one's life were learned at that conference.

In this chapter I will mention some of them and some of my own efforts to accept and honor my own anger. Several people have shared their struggles and/or their victories with me; I have included a few of their stories.

Believe It Or Not

Let's repeat once again. Anger is an emotion, a feeling. It is something that we live with, but we do not have to let it dominate us. Anger really has to be judged on what we do with it. Do we recognize it, accept it, honor it, and express it in a positive way? Or does our anger lie hidden and unresolved, unloved and ready to erupt at the slightest provocation?

Just before the Second World War, the Flying Tigers helped the Chinese fight the Japanese invaders. One day, a Flying Tiger ace had the worst cup of coffee he'd ever tasted. He was so angry that he jumped into his plane, took off, and found some enemy aircraft. He shot down several of them. His commanding officer was so impressed that he considered having that horrible coffee served each morning. That pilot really used his anger and its tremendous energy in a very forceful way. Thank God, it was against the enemy pilots and not against the cook.

What Were You Expecting?

One of the most helpful interventions at the A.C.T. conference on anger was by a participant who remarked, "Anger most often results if our expectations are not met. A very helpful step is to find out if our expectations were realistic or not." If they were unrealistic, we need to acknowledge that we were asking for more than we deserved or more than was possible. If our expectations were realistic, then we have a legitimate grievance. Both situations have to be resolved, but in different ways. When we are angry, we need to tell the truth to ourselves first before daring to correct anyone else. We start by asking ourselves whether our expectations of the other were realistic or not.

When we have realistic expectations which are not met by ourselves or by others, we need to express our anger. Most of us normally express anger at ourselves rather constructively and quite gently. There may be a lesson here. When angry at another, pretend you did the thing you find so provoking and see how you would want a friend to discuss the situation with you.

Personally, I think not many of us are very good at expressing anger at others, but we can learn. Not many of us were trained to confront anyone. We certainly feel anger, but often it is like a hot coal which we find very difficult to handle. It is there and it is causing us grief, but we don't know what to do with it.

Accept Your Anger And Honor It

Well, what are we going to do with our anger? First of all, we accept it as being there. It has a right to be honored. Then we do something about it. Many times that means we must be willing to confront the person with whom we are angry and discuss the situation. We need to admit any responsibility that we have for the situation and accept the other person's response. That does not mean the other will always cave in and apologize. Often there will be sharing of feelings and insights about the situation. Hopefully much of the heat will have gone out of the emotional response.

Have you ever read the rules for having a good fight in marriage? Some of them are obvious like: keep it current, keep it short. The last rule is: do something enjoyable with the other person. Close the door on the past and begin to rebuild the relationship. That's good advice in or out of marriage.

Some authors speak of three possibilities for handling one's anger:

1. suppression or repression; "keep the lid on and the emotion buried";

2. expression which is often explosive and even uncontrolled; "let it all come out no matter who gets hurt"; and

3. confession or expression to God and/or a spiritual friend for strength to handle it; "God, I'm so angry; help me."

Destructive Ways

The first possibility can destroy one's bodily health and peace while the second definitely destroys the peace and often the health of those around us.

Many people distrust and fear their anger so much that they even deny the emotion entirely on a conscious level, but it is still there and can explode with volcanic force in acts of irrational, even homicidal brutality. Examples are plentiful and painful. Two come to mind in which people who suppressed or repressed their anger exploded in a completely uncharacteristic rage. An all-American boy in a moment of rage stabbed his mother to death. The quiet long-suffering wife switched from carving the ham one day to driving the knife into her abusive husband's heart. Temporary insanity? Yes. But still great tragedy.

The second possibility is to express the anger without restraints and forget about the consequences. One man did that when he learned that his daughter was going to fail a subject and have to attend summer school. Screaming and yelling at a great rate were his initial reactions. Then, in the midst of his tirade, he realized that his pride was hurt because he'd have to admit to his friends that his daughter had to go to summer school. When that fact registered, he withdrew from his "pity party," calmed down, and helped her to face her situation by acting maturely himself.

The Constructive Way

The third method puts the Lord's healing power squarely in the middle of the situation and allows us to accept and honor our anger in and through him. This third way allows for the expression of anger, but adds the element of control by having the person turn to God and a spiritual friend for strength to handle it.

In my lifetime I've experienced all these methods for expressing anger. I'm getting better at the third method, although I do have a way to go. Believe me when I testify that the third method saves a lot of wear and tear on yourself and others. It certainly helps your physical as well as psychological and spiritual health.

Compassion

At a healing service sponsored by the Sacred Heart Institute, a speaker once said that her most natural emotion was anger. She tried to understand her anger. She tried to discover its source. Eventually, through prayer, she did just that. She also concluded that compassion was the remedy for her anger. When she would get angry at someone, she began to ask the Lord to give her a real sense of what was going on in the person and why the person had acted that way. She prayed for and received the gift of compassion.

Mother Theresa of Calcutta, while at the Eucharistic Congress in Philadelphia in 1976, was confronted in a very angry way by a TV interviewer. The person remarked, "Well, you're all right. You're very acceptable, and I like what you do. But what about the church, and what about all its wealth, and what about all its abuses?" The man went on to list all the so-called sins of the church in a very angry manner. Mother Theresa never even responded to the question, but said, "Oh, my, you seem to be so very angry. You don't seem to have much peace."

The man immediately changed and said, "Well, I am angry; but what do I do about it? How do I handle it?" Mother Theresa's response was, "You have to have faith." And the man's response was, "How do I get faith? I don't have any." She said, "Pray for it," and he responded, "I don't know how to pray."

Then with great simplicity, tenderness and compassion, very obviously loving this man who was so tormented, she said, "We will pray for you." And she did just that, praying for him right there. Very possibly only Mother Theresa and a few very holy people could ever have so quickly defused a situation so filled with anger and hatred of the church. But we can learn much by how she did it; by being herself, warm, loving, and very, very compassionate.

Take Your Anger To The Angry Jesus

Once while attending a workshop I became extremely angry at someone who betrayed a confidence. I tried several times and in various ways to handle my anger, but I needed help. During a healing service that evening I mentioned my anger to two people who were praying as a team. One of them remarked, "Now, Jerry, you're a very strong man. You feel things sensitively yet strongly. Anger can be a very good quality. You don't have to be afraid of it. There's tremendous energy there. Take your anger to the <u>angry</u> Jesus. Let the angry Jesus show you how to find the <u>gold</u> in your anger." What a marvelous help those few sentences were to me!

Pure Gold, Almost

About ninety percent of anger is a very positive thing. It's gold, and we're called upon to refine it and use it. Please read the story of Jesus' getting angry at the hypocrisy of the Pharisees in the Gospels. (Lk 11:37-53; Mt 23:1-39; Mk 7:1-16) Also read how he became angry because his Father's house had been turned into a den of thieves and then proceeded to cast the buyers and sellers out of the temple. (Mt 21:12-13; Mk11:15-18; Lk 19:45-48; Jn 2:13-17)

Notice how he used his anger. When you're angry, take it to the angry Jesus. Latch on to Jesus and ask him to guide you through your anger.

Ask him for the help to see the source of your anger and what you can do about it. Pray for compassion and holy boldness as you seek to express your anger constructively and use it as a brick to build up the kingdom of God.

I once drove a friend of mine, a religious sister, up to Boston so that she could register for graduate school. After she had made the necessary arrangements, she said that she'd like to stay overnight to be with her cousin. Although I knew it was supposed to snow, I said, "Fine."

I made arrangements to go out to dinner that evening with Sister, a priest from Boston College, and a parishoner with whom I was staying. We had a very enjoyable evening.

I also decided to go to a convent nearby to celebrate Eucharist the next morning. That was a very beautiful experience because a former grade school teacher of mine was in retirement there.

After Mass I went to pick up my colleague. It had snowed and it was rather slippery. At one traffic light I couldn't stop in time and I skidded into the car ahead of me. The driver jumped out of the car, saw that his car was fine, and said, "No problem." I whispered a "thank God" and drove on.

When I got out of my car at the apartment where Sister was staying, was I ever surprised to see how much damage had been done. I got so angry! My first thought was, "It's all her fault. She made me stay."

Then I caught myself because that was a lie. I had decided to stay at Sister's urging, but I had made the decision. I made arrangements to do things with the extra time. I decided and it was my responsibility. I very humbly and sincerely repented of trying to blame someone else.

A Time To Be Quiet
And A Time To Share

However, I was upset. When Sister came down, I mentioned the accident and said, "I need about five minutes to calm down." She said, "That's fine. I could use the prayer time anyway." So for five minutes we drove in silence and then very naturally started to talk. It was a very beautiful, prayerful and faith-filled experience for those four and a half hours driving back to New Jersey.

I always think of how I could have blown the whole experience by living the lie and not accepting my responsibility in the matter.

Again, I would challenge you to think about where your anger comes from and to be careful at whom you direct it. Realize that when you decide to do something, it's <u>your</u> decision and you're responsible for it. Try not to put the blame on someone else. It's perhaps the easiest thing in the world to do, but it's also one of the most dangerous things in the world for any relationship.

Love That Doesn't Give Up

A young man in his late teens had a disagreement with his family and walked out. In the beginning was his mother angry! Then she realized that her anger was doing no good for her, and it certainly wasn't helping her family. Definitely her anger was doing no good to the boy wherever he was.

So she began to say to Jesus each day: "He's baptized, he's yours, now you shepherd him, you watch over him." Then she sat down and wrote a love letter saying everything that she loved about this child of hers. She had no address to which to send it, but writing the letter cleared things up in her own mind. Somehow in the spiritual realm, the Holy Spirit was able to clear up something in the boy's mind also.

Then she realized there was more that she could do. She started to picture her son next to Jesus whenever she thought about him. She had been thinking about him often and in not too flattering terms. She kept a picture of her son next to one of Jesus, the Good Shepherd. Since she had these pictures in a prominent place she often saw them and so was reminded to pray even more earnestly.

A year after he left, her son called to say that he was all right and living on the West Coast. Just by coincidence (she felt it was by God-incidence) he had met some committed Christians. He had gone back to church and was finding a great deal of healing and love. He stayed on the West Coast for six more months and she was able to send him her love letter. The delay of over a year had only made it a more beautiful means of healing their relationship.

Finally he was reunited with his family, seeking forgiveness and ready to forgive. What a wonderful and moving reconciliation that was. A year and a half of constant prayer and of picturing her son with Jesus, the Good Shepherd, had paid handsome dividends. She thought it was worth it. How about you?

Is There Anger In Your Heart?

A priest once asked a very important question of a friend of mine who was going to the sacrament of Penance/Reconciliation. "Is there anger in your heart?" There was, and my friend experienced a great release from his unresolved and largely unexamined anger as he faced it and accepted it as his own. He honored it and invited Jesus into that area of his life. Needless to say, he was deeply touched and healed by that sacramental encounter with Jesus the Healer.

Prefer The Other

Another person was angry when one of the other speakers on a panel refused to have the discussion taped. While praying about the situation, my friend heard the words, "Prefer the other." He did just that and the Lord Jesus blessed him abundantly with an excellent talk and a remarkable healing.

Think about these last three stories. Each of them is true and, I think, has a lesson for all of us who must learn to accept, honor, and love our anger.

Please Consider This!

When angry, use the following three-line formula to express it:
> When you did (said) that
> I felt angry
> because ....

The first line lets the other know what he/she did or said. The second line lets you express your feeling of anger. The third line tells why you're angry and in your own words.

Practice using this formula in private before you try it with another as you will be awkward and embarrassed the first time. Practice will make it easier.

Or This . . .

Warren Molton gave a talk called "Friends, Partners, Lovers" on a cassette set <u>Two Become One, A Preparation For Marriage</u> (National Catholic Reporter Publishing Company, Kansas City, Missouri, 1977). In his talk he discussed the need to fight in a friendship and listed ten rules for such an encounter.

1. We have to get in touch with our feelings as quickly as possible, after any signal of being disturbed;

2. We ask the question, "What is the feeling?" We must name it. We acknowledge it to ourselves, claim it, own it.

3. We have to locate the source of the anger - who, when, where, how, why - simply and clearly.

4. Address your friend, privately if possible, and from the adult part of you. Say, "When you <u>did that</u> it made me feel angry. I want to discuss it with you."

5. Insist that your anger be honored for discussion, even if your friend feels it is inappropriate. Make him/her take your

feelings seriously.

6. Be fair. Listen to the feedback. Search for an explanation that satisfies both parties, not just excuses.

7. Get those feelings out. Talking about it should do it. If yelling is necessary, remember that this can greatly alarm those around you and can send further waves of pain through both of you and enflame your feelings even more.

8. Ask for and give forgiveness.

9. Contract to guard against the reoccurrence of that particular event.

10. Do something different. Take a walk, go to a movie, get out. Whatever you do, don't lock up the anger so that it becomes a cesspool that can continue to poison the relationship.

Tell It To Someone

A widow was grieving and boiling mad because she felt deserted and abandoned by old friends. She wrote:

"I have been a widow for almost two years and I wouldn't wish this life on a dog.

"Before my husband died he told me about two business deals he was making with a couple of friends. They were not in writing, merely oral agreements. My husband passed away before the deals were consummated.

"The two friends couldn't do enough for me. They included me in their plans, took me to places, and I was touched by their consideration.

"After the estate was settled I followed through on the two deals and paid both parties every cent. The minute the money was in their hands, the friends disappeared. I have not seen nor heard from them since.

"Don't tell me I did the right thing and that I should not regret it because now I can live with my conscience. It is just as hard to live with the bitter resentment that I feel."

The widow didn't write because she wanted advice. She wrote to unload her hostility. She felt better afterward because writing her letter seemed to put the whole situation into a very concrete perspective. After that she considered what her options were. She was too smart to wallow in bitter resentment for long. Gradually she let go of that negative sentiment and began to enjoy the blessings of her life. She made up her mind that two rotten apples weren't going to spoil her basket.

A Personal Story

A married couple once visited me while I was on vacation at the New Jersey shore. They had just had a fight, but didn't tell me. When we got to the beach on an overcast day, the woman started to cry and then the whole thing came out. I said a silent prayer: "Oh God, what am I going to do?"

Then the Lord spoke to me very clearly: "Put into practice what you have been writing about and do it now. I've sent these two to you just for that. Now get on with it!"

We were sitting on the beach, the man on the left, the woman on the right of me. Both were definitely turned away from each other. I told them to turn toward me and then we joined hands and began to pray.

I began by proclaiming that Jesus is and always will be Lord of all life and of the three of us gathered there. Then I prayed for freedom from every evil spirit of darkness, hatred, anger, and despair or anything else which needed to be cast out. I immediately prayed that the grace and light of the Holy Spirit would flow into them. The Lord suggested these words:

"Lord Jesus, you love these two more than I do. They are very special to me, but even more special to you. In faith and in trust I ask you now to touch and calm them, heal and love them into new life. You know their love for you and for me, your priest. By the power of that love and the priesthood you share with me, move into all the areas of their lives which need to be healed. But especially touch each of them where they are hurting at this moment."

As we prayed, I was earnestly asking the Lord to tell me what to do next. He had a plan but he wanted to get my attention and remind me that _he_ is the healer and I'm part of the team.

Depending on him each step of the way, we spent some time being quiet and then we prayed the "Our Father" and also the two prayers which follow it at Mass: the "Deliver us, o Lord" and the Prayer for Peace.

This was not the place nor time nor circumstances to have an embrace of peace, so we just continued to hold hands and to let the peace of Christ permeate every part of our beings. Then we let it flow through each of us to the others.

The sky had been overcast and cloudy, but as we sat and prayed, the sun broke through the clouds. That to me was a very hopeful and hope-filled moment.

As a "homework" assignment, I asked the two of them to write down as best they could what had gone on that morning and to let me know what they had been feeling. I wanted them to get in touch with the feeling tone of the whole experience. Then the three of us could see where God would have us look and pray for the healing they needed. I, for one, was sure he wanted to give them a special healing. In fact, I asked them to go on my faith and trust in the Lord when times got rough for them.

What did I learn from the whole experience?

1. Realize that Jesus is the only healer. On my own I can do nothing, but with him all things are possible.

2. Begin with prayer and stay in

prayer contact with the Lord all the way through it.

3. Know the power of the adversary and also the greater power of the Lord. Use the prayer of deliverance but always coupled with a prayer asking the Holy Spirit to fill the person(s) with light and grace.

4. Listen carefully to the promptings of the Lord. He is faithful and always will come through when you need him. Learn to wait trustingly for his movements.

5. Share your faith and trust with the other(s) as they may be sorely tested at that time and will have to lean on your faith and trust.

A Last Word

Why not try the following statements on for size? See how they strike you. Are they valid and meaningful in your life at this time?

I am responsible for my anger and what it is doing to me and to my health.

I am responsible for bringing my anger to the surface and for sharing it with the angry Jesus.

Concluding Prayer

Lord Jesus, thank you for being angry at times because I know I can bring my own anger to you. Help me to be honest in facing my anger. Help me to name it, own it, and share it with you. Teach me to put all that energy to work for you and for my brothers and sisters. And, Lord, show me how to be compassionate as you were. Thank you for giving me this great emotion of anger with its tremendous energy and power to help build up your kingdom.

RECAPITULATION

In this section we have been discussing the two very powerful emotions of fear and anger. Their power or raw energy often frightens people. After reading the two chapters in this section, I hope that you have gotten the message that these emotions have power to heal as well as to harm. Integrating our fears and our anger into our lives is a great part of coming to human Christian maturity. This is done <u>not</u> <u>without</u> <u>pain</u> and <u>never</u> <u>without</u> <u>Jesus</u>.

Remember that Jesus, especially during his agony in the garden, experienced fear of what was about to happen to him. He overcame that fear when he said, "If it be possible, let this chalice pass from me. Yet not my will, but yours be done." He knew the secret of overcoming fear by standing firmly in the will of his father. That's our best approach also. We face our fears with Jesus, we look through them with Jesus, and we surrender them to Jesus who shares with us his Father.

As we try to live our lives, there are times when we will be angry and that is good and holy. Our challenge is to be angry and to sin not. At such times we need to face our anger and honor it by sharing it with the angry Jesus. The angry Jesus will show us how to face our anger, honor it, and express it. With him we will be able to move through it and beyond it to compassion. That is the royal road to healing of anger.

SECOND SECTION

Introduction

In this section we look at grief in its many dimensions. Grief is an emotion which is rarely absent from our lives. Grief comes in its ordinary everyday form and definitely affects our world. In its extraordinary manifestations (death, divorce, serious illness) grief can, at times, shake our world to its foundations.

Since our lives are daily touched by grief in its various forms, we need to learn how to grieve in a way which is truly human and Christian.

Basically the lesson which we hope to learn is how to grieve, not in isolation but in union with others. We will learn how to grieve in company with Jesus, his mother, and his saints.

We will also learn about grief from our brothers and sisters who have experienced it in its various forms and its various intensities.

In this particular section we consider what grief is, how it affects the various stages and seasons of our lives; and we share some ways of healing it. This is not a "how to do it" chapter, although there are elements of that. It probably is best described as a "with whom to share your burden" chapter.

The Lord is close to the brokenhearted;
and those who are crushed in spirit
he saves.

Psalm 34

CHAPTER IV

GRIEF: A TIMELY GRACE
Let It Out So That You Can Let It Go

"Near the cross of Jesus there stood his mother, his mother's sister, Mary the wife of Clopas, and Mary Magdalene. Seeing his mother there with the disciple whom he loved, Jesus said to his mother, 'Woman, there is your son.' In turn he said to the disciple, 'There is your mother.' From that hour onward, the disciple took her into his care."(Jn 19:25-27)

A later volume in this series may treat of this subject more exhaustively, and I have also discussed various aspects of it in my book Birth to Birth. What I'd like to do in this chapter is give a good working definition of grief, and describe some of its aspects. Then I'll share with you some of the things the Lord has been teaching me about grief, grieving, mourning, bereavement, etc.

Grief is deep intense sorrow which encompasses great distress of body, mind and spirit. Sorrow is occasioned by the ordinary disappointments, losses, and regrets of life. Grief is a special sorrowing caused by the loss of a "significant other," be that a person, animal, job, place, thing, or part of one's body. Grief is much more acute and lasting than sorrow and is often accompanied by strong passionate displays of other feelings.

Grieving has been described very thoroughly in a leaflet published by Kairos. This leaflet is very helpful because of its depth and wisdom and because both are expressed in brief and simple terms.

"Grieving is to be in sorrow, to lament, feel distress, to mourn. Grieving is a process of sorrowing deeply over a period of time, experiencing deep sadness.

"Grieving is a series of painful experiences into which one enters and lives for a period of time before there is healing.

"Grieving is something like vomiting, coming and going in spasms, lurking for a time before erupting again and again and again.

"Grieving may produce feelings of fear, anger, great regret, guilt, shame, an abiding sense of uselessness, loneliness, an inability to focus, a desire to die.

"Grieving eventually ends because we only have so much capacity to carry sorrow and because we are also able to gather new resources for living.

"There is no right or wrong way to grieve. Each of us grieves in our own way which is right for us."[1]

S. Scott Sullender sees grief as an emotion with several distinct qualities. He became aware of these during his years in

parish and pastoral care ministries. He describes grief as:
1. dangerous;
2. complex;
3. subtle; and
4. powerful.

Grief can be <u>dangerous</u> to one's health and life. How often does the death or loss of a "significant other" lead to the subsequent death or serious illness of a relative or friend?

Grief is a <u>complex</u> emotion. One significant loss can affect many areas of the person's life and also have ramifications in the lives of others as well.

How <u>subtle</u> is grief? It is a part of most changes, even those that are quite positive moves. We grieve over what has to be left behind (home, friends, relatives, familiar surroundings, medical personnel), even as we rejoice.

Grief has <u>power</u> and it will not be submerged for long by a burst of activity. Sooner or later it demands to be felt, accepted, honored, and healed.2

Grieving Is O.K.

Are those who do not openly mourn better than those who do? Are the former to be held up as examples of Christian virtue? No way! Comments such as the following don't express a balanced view of grief/mourning.

"Isn't she brave! She hasn't even cried!"

"Isn't he strong? He hasn't even shed a tear or missed a day's work."

Those comments represent stoicism, not Christianity. Does mourning show a lack of faith in the love and power of God? Not at all. Do those who mourn have something wrong with their spiritual life which should be "straightened out"? Definitely not.

We are a unity of body, mind, and spirit and have become accustomed to the presence of loved ones in all those dimensions. When someone we love leaves us, we experience sorrow and grief. That's good, healthy Christian living.

Jesus himself experienced deep sorrow and wept over the death of Lazarus, the future destruction of Jerusalem, and his own sufferings and death. (Mt 26:36 - 46; Mk 14:32 - 42; Lk 19:41 - 44; Lk 22:39 - 46; and Jn 11:1 - 44) Why should we who follow Christ be any different?

Let us help one another to grieve, to be with one another in sorrow, to love one another as Christ loves us.

A Growth Stage

Grief and all that goes with grieving can be a real growth stage in life. We learn many lessons as we grieve. We learn to let go and to trust in God. Many people have testified to the growth that they have seen in themselves as they have worked through the grieving process. They now have a deeper appreciation of the great sources of strength within them. They have been tested and proved to be quite strong. But remember, not without pain. In such cases those testifying agree that the gain has been well worth the pain.

Would they have chosen to grow in quite this way? No! But with hindsight they see how God has worked in them, strengthened them and supported them.

Consider this one of those times when you should reward yourself for a job well done. A pat on the back, a kind word, or whatever reward is most appropriate will have a very good emotional effect. Hopefully, the reward will not be too fattening, illegal, or anything like that.

A Waiting Time

In any grieving process time is an essential part of the healing. A Neopolitan saying puts it succinctly: <u>Love makes time pass; time makes love pass</u>. I would suggest that time makes many other emotions besides love pass or fade away.

Father Henri Nouwen in his two cassette series "The Spirituality of Waiting"[3] discusses how we humans wait for God and how God waits for us. The first part of his talk uses the first two chapters of Luke's Gospel to show how we (in the persons of Mary and Joseph, Zechariah and Elizabeth, Simeon and Anna) wait for the Lord to fulfill his promise to send a Messiah. The last chapters of Luke show us how <u>God waits</u>

<u>for</u> <u>us</u> in the person of Jesus Christ as he undergoes his passion, death, and resurrection.

"The Word is what heals us. We wait for the Word to become flesh in us, to touch and inform us. Are we willing to let the Word reform and heal us? Simone Weil said: 'Waiting patiently in expectation is the foundation of the spiritual life.' Am I open to the Word which wants to address me? Can I stay tuned to the Word standing with trust in the presence of God? Can I persevere in my attitude of active waiting and expectation?"

How fearful we people of the last decade and a half of the 20th century are! War, nuclear power, drugs, crime, and many personal problems confront and frighten us. At times they paralyze us. Fearful people have a very hard time waiting. Actually, that's why waiting is not a very popular feeling for most of us.

Some questions come to mind which we have to answer sooner or later . . . and sooner would be better.

Can you stay with the pain?

Can you let the pain be there and endure it?

Can you trust that there's something new being born?

Can you wait long enough to be healed?

Entering into the pain means not running away from it or getting lost in a premature burst of activity. Why? Because we perceive, even if dimly, that what we have lost in a way is not just lost but will begin to take new shape in us even as we endure the pain itself. In the process we grow toward a new maturity.

Nostalgia

At times the grieving person can only think of the good things that the other did. There is a tendency to romanticize the past and to forget about some of the agony. I am not suggesting that we concentrate on the bad parts of a relationship, but rather that we strive to maintain some sort of balance. It probably wasn't as good as we remember it. On the other hand, it might not have been as bad either. More than likely, it was a mixture of good and bad. Time and waiting in faith will restore the balance and then we can rejoice in all that was good in the one for whom we grieve.

Grieving is often about a place which we have left where we knew security, love, and warmth in an extended family. It was home for us and now we have to leave it and it hurts. In my own life I grieved for my home town after we had moved away. I definitely romanticized the place. When my grandmother died just as I was going to college, I found out that the attachment was not to the place, but it was to her. She, by living there, had made the place meaningful. My other relatives had a supporting role, but she was definitely the main interest and attraction.

Think about the possibility in your own life that you have grieved over one thing, but in reality it was for something else. You may seem to be grieving for a thing or place, when in reality you are grieving for a person or even for a dream that person embodied. We often grieve for a broken relationship and it seems to be for the person involved. But when we think about it, we realize we are grieving for our dream of what the relationship could have been. Our dreams got all wrapped a-around the other person and soon we could not tell them apart.

Remember that grief is a dangerous, complex, subtle, and powerful emotion. When grieving we need to take the time and effort to
    identify it,
      name it,
        and
          face it.
Only in that way can we recover from it. Recovery is possible, <u>but not without pain</u>. However, healing and recovery are worth the pain.

Recovery Is Possible

What are some signs that a person is recovering from the intense stage of grief and grieving?

    1. The person honestly mourns, weeps, laments, moans, resents, and even hates doing whatever is necessary to break the emotional freeze to ventilate all feelings

of distress.

2. The person surrenders to the painful reality of the separation, unconditionally accepting the fact that there is no turning back while turning one's life over to God who leads the way out of the valley.

3. The person is able to ask for help and to use it.

4. The person begins to see that recovery is a process requiring time and trust . . . trust that recovery is possible and that God who is faith is with him/her on each stage of the recovery journey.

5. The person chooses with God's help to do what is necessary to recover.

6. The person discovers that willpower does not work for recovery, that only surrender does and that recovery is a growth process beginning and continuing with the exercise of gratitude.

7. The person is able to express gratitude to God for all gifts and mercies given.

8. The person decides to reclaim life and to live it as fully and happily as possible.

9. The person is able to attend to the necessary details of life and living.

10. The person develops a new sense of self satisfaction in things accomplished. He or she learns to "munch" the fruits of any victories.4

Grieving and Relationship

Grieving over a relationship is comparable to what Kubler-Ross has said about a person facing death and going through the five stages. These are denial, anger, bargaining, depression and finally acceptance.

There is a <u>denial</u> that it's over. "This couldn't be happening to me." The relationship is changed/dead, and yet there is a tremendous yearning for it to return.

Then comes <u>anger</u> that it did happen. I am angry at this person and that person; my imagination runs wild. "I'll get even with him. Someday he'll want to come back and I'll spit in his face." "She'll be sorry. I was the best thing that ever happened to her. But she'll never see me again." "I hope I die, and then that so-called friend will regret how much he hurt me."

<u>Bargaining</u> comes next. "If she comes back, I'll change. I'll be more understanding. I won't insist on always getting my own way. I'll call more often. I'll do this; I'll do that."

<u>Depression</u> is the fourth stage. "I'm no good. No one loves me or understands me. I'm all alone."

<u>Acceptance</u> comes last, but certainly not least in importance. "Yes, the relationship is dead. It is not coming back to life. <u>I</u> <u>am</u> going on and I'm going to live and I'm going to make something of my life."

A necessary element in so much of this is to take the time and not opt for the instant fix. So many people get into another relationship on the rebound. A person has to experience the pain. Definitely don't drop one relationship only to flow right into another. See how you change for the better as you stand fast and move through the stage of grieving. <u>But not without pain</u>, we say again. Believe me, the gain will be worth it.

Grieving And Divorce

Grieving for a divorced person can be terribly real and potentially destructive. Some people maintain that it is more traumatic even than coping with the death of a loved one.

In the case of death of a spouse, one feels many things, but not necessarily such a sense of failure. In divorce, the sense of rejection and failure can be almost overwhelming. If your spouse left you, you have a constant reminder of rejection. Even if you were the person to leave the marriage, a sense of failure and defeat nags at you because you could not make it work. Sometimes you may be grieving because of the loss of "my first love." In other cases you may be grieving as a reaction to the loss of the "myth of marriage" or the fantasy of living and loving happily ever after in the vine covered cottage or condo.

Anger is also expressed at the Lord for letting the divorce happen. We say to God, "Why did this happen to me? I did everything right. I married a believer, did so in the Church, and gave my complete dedication to the marriage. We could have made it work if she or he had only tried even a little. So why didn't you <u>do</u> something, God? Why did this have to happen?'

This anger must be examined and the reason for the failure in the marriage determined. Hopefully, we will come to see that God did not cause the failure. He allowed it to happen and each of the partners contributed to the problems of selfishness, non-communication, lack of commitment, etc.

Self-esteem is greatly diminished by a divorce. Overcoming the loss of self-esteem and beginning to feel "good about oneself" is a very real stage of the healing process. Divorce can be a "growth" situation but this usually can only be appreciated after some time has passed. There is great need for support and encouragement before this happens.

Many churches are providing the personnel and the facilities to maintain support groups for the divorced. In the Archdiocese of Newark, New Jersey, there is an active and on-going ministry to divorced and separated Catholics.5 In its eight or nine years of existence, the ministry has helped many people through the grieving process of divorce. Not a small part of its efforts is devoted to clearing up a deep-rooted misunderstanding among our Catholic people regarding the status of the divorced person in the Church. Because of this misunderstanding, many of our brothers and sisters who are experiencing the crisis of divorce absent themselves from the Eucharist or even from the Church community as a whole. They do so at a time when they are in great need of the healing presence of the Lord and the support of the Christian community.

The position of the Church is very clear regarding the divorced: the divorced Catholic (who has not remarried without benefit of Church annulment) is entitled to full participation within the sacramental community of the Church. Thus, divorced persons not only are invited to continue to receive the sacraments of Reconciliation and Eucharist, but also may expect the Church to offer the healing presence of the Lord through the concern and support of its members.

With regard to those who divorce and remarry without an annulment, it is important that we be aware that in 1977 Pope Paul VI at the request of the American Bishops lifted the ban of excommunication imposed on divorced Catholics who have remarried. Pope John Paul II "called upon pastors and the whole community of the faithful to help the divorced and with solicitous care to make sure that they do not consider themselves as separated from the Church, for as baptized persons they can and indeed must share in her life."

What about annulments? An annulment is the process by which the local Bishop, after serious investigation, declares that a true marriage never existed because some essential element was lacking. Each diocese has a tribunal (court) to investigate the circumstances. If you or a friend is interested in getting an annulment, do something. Why not speak to a priest friend, one of your parish priests, your diocesan chancery office, or someone who has received an annulment. Don't be afraid to ask for help. It's available. The Catholic who has received an annulment is free to seek out a new partner and to enter into marriage with that partner. Be aware so that you are not taken by surprise that annulments, freeing though they are, also involve a grieving process.

It is understandable that questions may be raised in the minds of some Catholics as to how we can uphold the teaching of the Church regarding the permanence of marriage and at the same time reach out in love to those who have experienced divorce. It is important that we look to Jesus as our model and remember that all persons were welcome to walk with him, especially those who were troubled. The crisis of divorce brings much suffering into the families who experience it. To offer compassion and support to our divorced members in no way contradicts the Church's teaching regarding the permanence of marriage. In imitation of Jesus as Teacher, the Church calls people to live the ideal of a permanent marriage. In imitation of Jesus as compassionate Healer, the Church as a healing community reaches out to those who have not been able to live out that ideal.

Grieving For A Stage Of Life

Aging is another type of dying. Sometimes we refer to it as the "golden years."

I've heard people who were in those years scorn that particular phrase. They long for their youth again. In the poem <u>Desiderata</u> there is a line about gracefully letting go of the things of youth. That is an ideal and yet how difficult it is when the body begins to break down and there are more ailments than seemingly one individual can bear. There is a dichotomy between the very healthy older person and the ill one. One of the bishops has suggested that the Church mobilize the healthy ones to help the others. Those that are in good health can give thanks to God for that gift of good health by reaching out to those who are not as healthy. The process of letting go of youth and reaching middle age is often called the middle age crisis. One dies to dreams, to things one might have done, but didn't do.

    Nostalgia can so glowingly paint youth that we forget what adolescence really means. What a joy it is to see someone enjoying who he or she is and where and what he or she is. The constant longing to be someone else, to be a different age just takes away from what today might bring by way of joy.

    Another concept is to balance the joys with the sorrows of life, the failures with the successes. Beyond all of this and long after all of this has faded into vague memories, the person survives.

Grief And Addiction

The only way out of an addiction is <u>death</u>: death of the addict or death to the addiction. In either case, there is grieving a-plenty. There are so many addictive behaviors. In AA an important slogan is "One drink is too many; a thousand are not enough." The slogan gets across the truth that for an addictive person, alcohol is a poison. They are allergic to it in a deadly way. Alcoholism is a progressive terminal disease. Other addictions may also be progressive terminal diseases and they cannot be healed or at least controlled if one continues to feed them literally (one drink or bite) or figuratively. Food or sexual addictions may also be the hardest of all addictions because it's very unlikely that anyone of us is ever going to cut away completely - figuratively or literally - our sexuality or our need for food.

An addict needs to accept his or her powerlessness over the addiction and should think about joining a program of spiritual recovery along the lines of one of the twelve-step programs such as Alcoholics Anonymous, Overeaters Anonymous, Sexaholics Anonymous, etc. Check the telephone book for the various self-help groups. Alcoholics Anonymous is a good start and its office personnel are invariably very helpful and well-informed about the other self-help and twelve-step programs.[6] I highly recommend most twelve- or fourteen-step programs.[7]

Most recovery programs are much more effective when combined with inner healing prayer which has been discussed in the first volume of this series. Making contact with a spiritual director and allowing him or her to make the journey with the addict to healing and wholeness in the Lord Jesus usually accelerates the recovery process.

Grief And Sickness

A man had been enormously active in social justice. He had built houses for the poor and was active in politics and in all causes to better the country and the world. When he was fifty he discoverd that he had cancer. It got progressively worse and soon he was confined to bed. When Father Henri Nouwen visited him the friend said, "Here I am in this bed and I don't even know how to think about being sick. My whole way of thinking about myself is in terms of action, doing things for people. And now I can't do anything for others."[8]

What the friend wanted was help to think about the situation in a new way because not being active anymore was almost driving him to despair. He, like many others, had always thought of himself as having worth and meaning mainly because of what he did for others. His plea was, "I don't know how to be sick. I don't know how to think about dying. Please, come and help me face these circumstances."

Not only couldn't the man do anything for others anymore, but now almost everything was being done to him and for him. He no longer had control over his own body. In that context, Henri and he read a book which treated the Agony in the Garden and the Passion of Jesus. As they read, they realized that Jesus had been "handed over" into the hands of his enemies. Some translations say "betrayed," but the Greek word means "to be handed over." The same word is used to describe how God <u>handed Jesus over</u>. God did not hesitate <u>to hand over</u> his only begotten Son to suffer in order to redeem us from sin and evil. The "handing over" of Jesus divides his life into two parts. For most of his life Jesus was active in preaching, teaching, and healing. He travelled up and down the countryside, influencing the people and institutions of his time. In the second part of his life, after he had been "handed over" to his enemies, he became the one to whom things were being done. He was beaten, scourged, mocked, judged, treated cruelly, and finally killed on the cross.

Jesus did not fulfill his vocation as Savior just by what he did, but also by what he allowed to be done to him. It was a matter of "Passion vs. Action" - being the recipient of other people's actions versus acting and influencing their lives.

At that stage of his life, Jesus offered people a choice to be his disciples or his executioners. And then he had to wait for them to make the choice. His agony in Gethsemane occurred not only because he had to die, but also because he had to wait for people to make their choices whether to betray him or follow him.

Questions

What does all that say to you about your concept of who you are?
Are you able to define yourself only in terms of what you do rather than who you are?
Do you know who you are?
Do you realize that Jesus still waits for people to make their choices to be his disciples or his executioners?
What in your own life and history will help you face sickness and the very real grieving over your diminished physical power and control?

Pause To Consider

There comes a time in asking the Lord to heal us or someone else when we need to pause and consider carefully the whole situation. We need to pray for discernment and wisdom and the answers to some questions.
Is there anything preventing the healing from taking place such as lack of forgiveness?
Is the Lord asking that we persevere in prayer no matter what seems to be happening?
If there is not to be a physical healing, are we to pray for something else?
Is this person called to redemptive

suffering, to share the cross of suffering with Jesus?

The answers to such questions do not come easily or quickly. Don't rush to conclusions. Take your time and consult your spiritual director and/or other mature people, especially those who have walked with the Lord for a long time and who have the gift of discernment. Redemptive suffering is a more common vocation than we might imagine, but it isn't to be presumed. Those who are critically or terminally ill often hear this call and heed it.

If, in fact, it seems that we are called to be a companion to the suffering Christ by our illness or injury, perhaps this poem may express something of value for that special graced moment.

Suffering In Union With Jesus

Your cross, my Lord, has now been offered me.
I accept, but we both know how weak I am -
I am so frightened by the burden and the pain.
I accept the cross, my Lord, because it is yours
And you will not let me carry it alone.
Your strong shoulders will strengthen my weakened frame.

You are the Lord of my life, my brother, my savior, my constant companion.

You will heal me of that fear which only intensifies my pain.
You would heal me of my illness if it were for my gain.
I ask no more; for I hear your call to the cross.
And I know that with you and in you I am now called
To help save our world, more desperately in need of health than I.

My prayer, my brother, is a simple one.
Be with me and in me during all the days to come.
Give me more joy than pain to bear.
More happiness than sadness, more truth than doubt.
More hope than desolation, more vitality than boredom.
Finally, my brother, may my soul and spirit be vibrant with health.

I accept the cross of my illness, but in your love
I know that you will not allow that cross to come alone.
These are the conditions of my covenant with you, Lord.
For what I truly want is what you, too, seek.
I want more life than death, a life beyond all death.
A life which does not die, a life with you, my Lord.9

Grief And Dying

Grief is most often associated with the death of a loved one. How few of us ever take the time to prepare for that event!

A cancer specialist once contrasted cancer with a fatal heart attack. The latter closes the door on reconcilation and healing with loved ones, while the former, although a great physical evil, at least offers time for these things. In that sense, the specialist viewed cancer as not entirely evil and useless. Cancer patients are given time to prepare for death, to reconcile broken relationships, to seek forgiveness and to give it where needed.

But why wait for cancer, a heart attack, or whatever? Why not take the time to think about death, your own or that of a loved one?

The following excerpt from <u>Birth to Birth</u> may be helpful. Please, read it prayerfully and reflectively. Why not discuss it with the Lord and/or a friend?

"Your life begins and ends with birth.

"You are born to live, and yet to die someday. You are born to die, and yet live forevermore.

"You have many births, but two are crucial. The first is that traumatic experience when you are expelled from your mother's womb, and slapped into breathing, yelling, struggling life. The second is equally traumatic; for by it you are torn from the womb of this life and plunged into the mysterious existence of the next life.

"In each birth, <u>you</u> are born. You, unique and inexpressible, survive and thrive, developing the countless facets and qualities of your personality.

"Death must be faced. How you face the problem of death and the outcome of that confrontation will determine not only your view of death but even more so your view of life. In the process, much will be said about how to live this life abundantly.

"Death is a phenomenon which provokes a whole gamut of emotions: fear, anger, resentment, frustration and futility; or joy, acceptance, peaceful resignation, hope and faith in the Lord who is stronger than death.

"You and I will one day have to pass through death to a new life in God's country - our true homeland.

"May you learn to react affirmatively to death as the new birth and to strengthen your belief in the risen, healing Lord who calls you to the fullness of life."10

What To Do To Be Of Comfort

<u>Stay around after</u> the funeral, divorce, loss has occurred. Friends and relatives have a tendency to get absorbed into their own activity and concerns. Many grieving people lift their heads only to find themselves deserted. "Where did everyone go? What happened? Why is no one around? Did I do something wrong? I feel

like a leper."

Honor the pain and don't try to fix it. Grief is a painful emotion. There must be pain before there can be healing. Allowing one who grieves to experience the pain and to walk through it to healing is a noble though admittedly frustrating way of loving one's neighbor. Permit the bereaved to live his/her own pain. It is one thing to sorrow with a person, but quite another thing to interfere with the pain.

Don't forget your heart. Grieving is a matter of the heart rather than the head. Listen to the feelings of the bereaved, permitting the sorrow to surface and the pain to be openly expressed. Invite all feelings to surface and listen through the silences. Your being there is more important than saying the right word.

Don't play God. People who have experienced a loss often feel cheated by God or others. Accept all expressions of grief, including anger, shame, guilt, and resentment. Let the bereaved be angry at God and express it to you. Elizabeth Kubler-Ross used to tell her students not to worry about God because he could handle any anger sent his way.

Let the bereaved talk openly about the departed loved one or of what has been lost. This is a vital part of the healing process. Don't always switch to some more pleasant (safer) topic.

Hang in there. Grieving takes time. Some authorities estimate that when death has been expected the bereavement period generally lasts approximately six months, whereas with an unexpected death it may take longer, up to thirteen months and more. That's just a rough estimate, but let it alert you to the possible duration of the grieving time. Regardless of how long it takes, hang in there with the person until the grieving subsides. Be aware that it will cycle back again. Friends need to know that there is an ebb and flow to grieving. And that's o.k. because each time grief's power will lessen. If not, it may become obvious that the grief is "hooked" on to something else which is keeping it alive. Grief can hook into feelings of rebellion, rejection, abandonment, fear, and guilt, etc. In such cases, the grieving person needs help from a competent professional.

    <u>Don't</u> <u>fake</u> <u>it</u>. Don't promise to be around if you are not interested in being there, or can't be there. If you do promise but you can't fulfill the commitment, let the person know what's happening in your life. Promise what you can deliver and then do it or explain why you can't.11

Less Obvious Griefs

We have been discussing obvious grief - cases of grief which are easily perceived and momumental in impact. There are other less obvious but still very real areas of grief. These are even at times quite subtle in their effect, but dangerous nonetheless. Some of us don't even know that we are grieving at times, but we are aware that something is going on within us.

When that happens, try to get in contact with those feelings or vague rumblings within. See if perhaps they are not connected with some loss, then name the loss, be aware of what it is and how you are reacting. This holds true in your own case and also with those who are part of your life.

Just A Reminder

Grief is the human emotional response to love. Love comes in an infinite variety of forms. It can refer to people, places, objects, relationships, bodily organs, even ideas, dreams and goals. In addition, grief may be triggered in response to an anticipated or perceived loss, as well as to actual losses.

First, grief itself is a process and, therefore, it is always changing and becoming. Grief is never a fixed commodity. Grief is itself different at different stages in its process. Second, grief varies with the type of loss involved. The grief over the death of a loved one is not the same as grief over the loss of a job or a prized pet or possession. The type of loss colors the type of grief. Third, grief reactions vary widely with the unique individuals involved. Variables such as age, sex, religious beliefs, personality structure, and length and intensity of the relationship with the lost person or thing will vary with different cultural contexts. Even within one culture, various subcultures and family systems will mold the social expressions of grief. How a British gentleman expresses his grief will probably be worlds apart from the way a similar Iranian man would express his. In part, our culture helps to determine how we grieve.12

"One of my friends and colleagues suffered an unusual and grievous loss when he and his family were moving across country. They had everything they owned in a U-Haul truck, except for a few items in the family car tailing behind. One night, while sleeping in a motel somewhere in the great midwest, the truck was stolen. They awoke the next morning to find it gone - completely gone, vanished! Everything they owned was gone. Later the police located the truck - empty, of course. Everything that they had accumulated over years - the favorite easy chair, the family mementos, the children's toys, all of their clothes (other than the suitcase in the car), the family records - were all lost. At the moment of loss, they were involved already in a loss experience. A few days earlier they had said good-bye to their family home, friends, colleagues and jobs. Now their grief was compounded and intensified by the loss of all their material possessions. Particularly painful to them was the loss of the family picture albums. 'It seems cruel,' they noted. 'What would burglars do with such albums? They'd probably just throw them somewhere in a ditch.' Suddenly their family history had vanished. 'We lost more than the material things,' they went on. 'It was a loss of identity, history, and our roots as a family.'

"My friend's experience, while unusual in the way it happened, is similar to that kind of loss associated with natural disasters. Natural disasters, such as fires, earthquakes, floods, etc., can be just as total in their scope. Often these disasters involve the loss of friends and family members as well as the wholesale loss of material possessions. This kind of grief, therefore, can be totally engulfing and all-consuming. Further, such losses often strike without warning - suddenly in the night. J.S. Tyhurst has studied the individual emotional reactions to various kinds of disasters. He has isolated a three-stage process: impact, recoil and post-traumatic. He has labeled as 'disaster syndrome' the elements of the process: guilt, recurring fears of catastrophic experience, emotional withdrawal, and psychosomatic illness. The disaster syndrome is an example of a type of grief reaction, compounded by the unusual comprehensiveness and suddenness of the loss."[13]

Grief Exercise
A Scripture Meditation

Imagine yourself standing at Calvary beneath the cross of Jesus. Mary his mother is on your left and John, the beloved disciple, is on your right. They have welcomed you into their group. You feel very much a part of them and you share their sorrow and even horror at what is happening to the Lord. And yet, you stand there filled with a deep sense of faith and love as well as that sense of sorrow and pain.

Now is the time to face your own grief. Don't deny or dismiss it, but rather own it and accept it as both the fact and feeling it is.

Slowly stretch out your arms to the cross - to Jesus on the cross. Open your hands and hold up to Jesus your grief and what caused it. Imagine Jesus wrenching his hands free of the nails and reaching down to accept your burden. He takes it gently and places it against his heart. Through swollen lips he gently and lovingly speaks.

"I will share your grief. I will help you to face it and the pain it brings. I will give you strength to stay with the pain until healing comes. Together we will look forward to resurrection. I will never leave you alone. I will never desert you. This is my solemn oath to you."

Concluding Prayer

Some emotions are too intimate and personal to be expressed in another person's prayer. Your own response in words or actions, in the movements of your heart or mind is the concluding prayer for this chapter. Be at peace.

FOOTNOTES

1. Box 24306, Minneapolis, Minnesota.
2. S.Scott Sullender, *Grief and Growth* (New York: Paulist Press, 1985), pp. 1-3.
3. The Modern Cassette Library, Ave Maria Press, Notre Dame, Indiana 46556.
4. Kairos.
5. The local parish or diocesan chancery office would know details about such ministries in your area.
6. You may also write to: Alcoholics Anonymous World Services, Inc., Box 459, Grand Central Station, New York, NY 10163.
7. Homosexuals Anonymous has fourteen steps and is a very openly Christ-centered approach. For information, write: H. A. Fellowship Services, P.O. Box 7881, Reading, PA 19603.
8. From Nouwen's tapes, "A Spirituality of Waiting."
9. Ruane, *Birth to Birth*, p. 33.
10. Ibid., pp.vii-viii.
11. Kairos.
12. Sullender, pp. 24-25.
13. Ibid., p. 17.

RECAPITULATION

We have seen how grief is a part of every stage and season of our lives. Grief is a dangerous, complex, subtle and powerful emotion but be not afraid. Others have grieved before us and have taught us much about it.

We need to <u>indentify</u> the presence of grief in our lives, <u>name</u> it, and <u>face</u> it, but not in isolation. Ask Jesus, Mary and the saints to accompany you. Don't hesitate to seek help from your brothers and sisters in God's family.

Remember, recovery and healing are possible, not always according to our plans and timetables, but according to God's. We can place our trust in him. We can place all our cares upon him because he cares for us.

Moved with compassion
   Jesus touches and heals us.

CONCLUDING REMARKS

The portion of the healing journey charted in this book is ending. Our own personal healing journey continues.

Enjoy yours as I plan to enjoy mine. Remember: don't run over the flowers but stop not only to smell but to touch, paint, sketch, talk or sing to the flowers. Who cares what anyone thinks?

To tell the truth, we probably still do care, but we will solve the situation differently now. Why not invite others to join us? At the least, we can share some comments on the beauty of what we are finally seeing and touching.

When the going gets tough, and it will at times, just look at the picture of Jesus on the opposite page. Let his compassionate love touch and heal you. Walk into his arms and know the freedom of sharing your life and all its stages and seasons with your loving Lord.

I continue to pray that this series and especially this volume will bless you and will offer light and comfort as you continue prayerfully - and also playfully - on your healing journey to emotional health, to living life more abundantly.

> Gerald Patrick Ruane
> Caldwell, New Jersey
> November 1, 1986

APPENDIX A

Sacred Heart Institute
Audio Cassettes

__Healing And Emotions__
  Healing and Your Emotions
  Healing and Fear
  Healing and Anger
      Rev. Gerald P. Ruane
  Healing and Grief
      Sister Ruthann Williams, O.P.
  Healing and Guilt
      Sister Lois Curry, O.P.

__Loved Into Healing And Wholeness__
  A Vision for God's People
  Growing In Intimacy With Jesus
  Healing the Whole Self
      Abbot David Geraets, O.S.B.

__Healing In General__
  Healing (5 short talks)
  Homilies and Reflections on Healing
  The Power of God's Love
  Rededication to God
  Overcoming Obstacles To Healing
      Rev. Gerald P. Ruane

__Healing And Loving Yourself__
  Living In God's Light and Truth
      Rev. Gerald P. Ruane
  Self-Worth: Loving Yourself
  Accepting Self: Freedom from a Negative Self-Image
      Sister Lois Curry, O.P.

Healing Fears And Weaknesses
- Fears, Faith and Focus
- The Spirit of Pentecost: Healing Fears and Weakness
- Freedom from the Orphan Within
  - Rev. Gerald P. Ruane

Living The Healed Life
- Healing and Twelve-Step Programs
- Discipline and the Christian Life
- Intimacy with Jesus through Scripture
- Bearing One Another's Burdens
- Election: Chosen, Gifted and Touched
  - Rev. Gerald P. Ruane
- Letting Go
  - Dr. Marie Gatza
- Healing through the Book, the Bread, and the Brothers and Sisters
- Virtues, Fruits and Gifts of the Holy Spirit
- Self-Reflection: Pathways to Under-Standing
  - Sister Lois Curry, O.P.
- Response: Compassion Toward a Hurting World
  - Sister Ruthann Williams O.P.

Mary, Mother of God
- Mary: Her Role in Healing
  - Rev. Gerald P. Ruane and Bud Earley
- Mary: Model of Faith
  - Rev. Gerald P. Ruane and Barbara Shlemon

<u>Music for Contemplative Listening</u>
 The Carpenter
   Father Jack McGinnis
 I Love You, My People
   Bob Cloutier

APPENDIX B

Professional Healing Organizations

The Association of Christian Therapists
    725 Bayview Avenue
    Clearwater, Florida 33520
    813-797-4030

The membership of the Association of Christian Therapists (A.C.T.) is made up of men and women in health and mental health fields who have made a radical commitment to Jesus Christ as personal Savior and Lord. The membership, which is international, seeks to give glory to God and to serve others by prayerfully integrating God's Word for healing with exemplary professional care.

The Order of Saint Luke
    P.O. Box 13701
    San Antonio, Texas 78213

The Order of Saint Luke is an international and interdenominational organization committed to the commission of Jesus to preach, teach, and heal, specifically as regards restoring the ministry of healing to the church universal. The Order promotes the practice of holding Healing Services, promoting a sound pastoral and counseling ministry and works to develop support groups in many areas. Laity and clergy are invited to join.

APPENDIX C

Further Reading

Agundo, Philomena
  Affirming the Human Body and the Holy
  Whitinsville, MA: Affirmation Books, 1979
Baaken, Kenneth L.
  The Call to Wholeness
  New York: Crossroad Publishing, 1985
Baars, Conrad W., M.D.
  Feeling and Healing Your Emotions
  Plainfield, NJ: Logos, 1979
Beecher, Willard and Marguerite
  Beyond Success and Failure
  New York: Pocket Books, 1966
Beesing, Maria, Patrick H. O'Leary, and Robert J. Nogosek
  The Enneagram
  Denville, NJ: Dimension Books, 1984
Breault, William, S.J.
  A Voice Over The Water
  Notre Dame, IN: Ave Maria Press, 1985
Carnes, Patrick
  Out Of The Shadows
  Minneapolis, MN: Compcare Pubs., 1983
Groeschel, Benedict J.
  The Courage To Be Chaste
  Ramsey, NJ: Paulist Press, 1985
Hauser, Richard J.
  In His Spirit
  Ramsey, NJ: Paulist Press, 1982
Herbstrith, Waltraud
  Edith Stein: A Biography
  San Francisco: Harper & Row, 1985

Holm, Norma and Paul
    The Runner's Bible
    Boston: Houghton Mifflin, 1943
Kelsey, Morton
    Discernment: A Study in Ecstacy & Evil
    New York: Missionary Society of St. Paul, 1978
Lacey, Maryanne
    An Invitation to Healing
    Yonkers, NY: House of Peace, 1985
Linn, Matthew and Dennis
    Healing Life's Hurts
    Ramsey, NJ: Paulist Press, 1978
    Healing the Greatest Hurt
    Ramsey, NJ: Paulist Press, 1985
    _____ with Sheila Fabricant
    Prayer Course for Healing Life's Hurts
    Ramsey, NJ: Paulist Press, 1983
    Praying with One Another for Healing
    Ramsey, NJ: Paulist Press, 1984
Maloney, George, S.J.
    Nesting in the Rock
    Denville, NJ: Dimension Books, 1977
Mannin, Ethel
    Late Have I Loved Thee
    Garden City, NY: Doubleday Inc., 1948
Manning, Brennan, T.O.R.
    The Wisdom of Accepted Tenderness
    Denville, NJ: Dimension Books, 1978
Muggeridge, Malcolm
    Something Beautiful For God
    New York: Random House, 1971
McDonald, Robert, M.D.
    Memory Healing
    Atlanta, Crossroad Books

MacNutt, Francis, O.P.
    The Power To Heal
    Notre Dame, IN: Ave Maria Press, 1977
Norwood, Robin
    Women Who Love Too Much
    New York: Pocket Books, 1985
Payne, Leanne
    The Broken Image
    Westchester, IL: Crossway Books, 1981
    Crisis In Masculinity
    Westchester, IL: Crossway Books, 1985
Ruane, Gerald P.
    Overcoming Obstacles To Healing
    Caldwell, NJ: Sacred Heart Press, 1985
    Birth to Birth
    Staten Island, NY: Alba House, 1976
Sanders, Carl J.
    Finding God Through Healing
    Nashville: The Upper Room, 1959
Shlemon, Barbara Leahy
    Healing the Hidden Self
    Notre Dame, IN: Ave Maria Press, 1982
Sheed, F. J.
    Death Into Life
    New York: Arena Letters, 1977
Stapleton, Ruth Carter
    The Experience of Inner Healing
    Waco, TX: Word Inc., 1977
Steindl-Rast, Bro. David
    Gratefulness at the Heart of Prayer
    Ramsey, NJ: Paulist Press, 1984
Sullender, S. Scott
    Grief and Growth
    Ramsey, NJ: Paulist Press, 1985
Viscott, David, M.D.
    The Language of Feelings
    New York: Arbor House, 1976